Frank George Carpenter

Travels through Asia with the Children

Frank George Carpenter

Travels through Asia with the Children

ISBN/EAN: 9783744756105

Printed in Europe, USA, Canada, Australia, Japan

Cover: Foto ©Andreas Hilbeck / pixelio.de

More available books at **www.hansebooks.com**

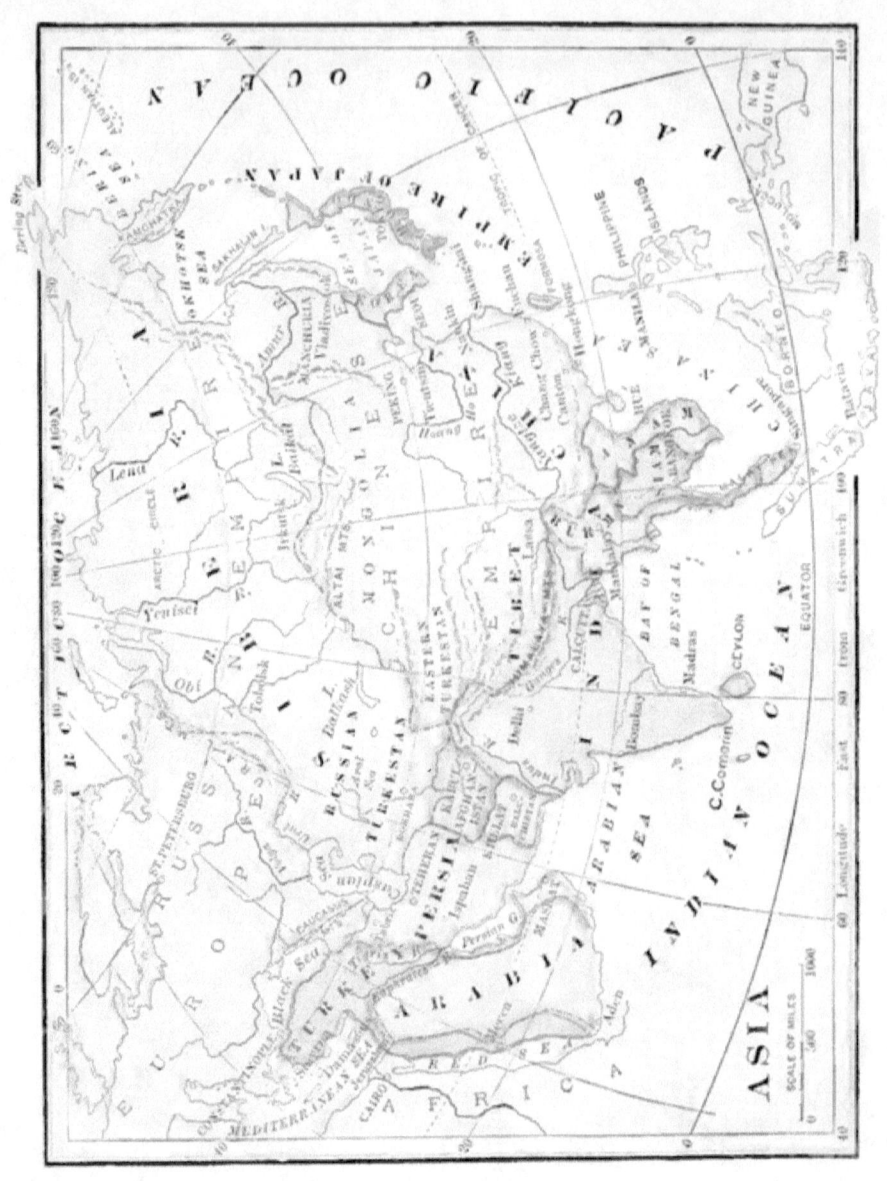

TRAVELS THROUGH

ASIA

WITH THE CHILDREN

BY

FRANK G. CARPENTER

NEW YORK ∴ CINCINNATI ∴ CHICAGO
AMERICAN BOOK COMPANY

PREFACE.

In writing this book, it has been the aim of the author to give a simple description of the peoples and countries of Asia as they exist to-day. To make this description interesting to young readers, he has taken them on an imaginary tour through the countries mentioned, and has presented to their view just those things which would naturally claim the attention of intelligent children. Having in mind both the entertainment and the instruction of his audience, he has anticipated their numerous questions concerning the strange things which they would encounter in their travels, and has endeavored to give them that sort of information which, while affording them pleasure, will at the same time add to their stock of useful knowledge.

Leaving America by the northern route across the Pacific, the children are conducted to Japan, where they make their first acquaintance with Asiatic life. Then they sail northward, visiting Korea and eastern Siberia, and then back around the Korean peninsula to the great Empire of China. After noticing the strange features of life and work among the Chinese, they sail southward from Hongkong to Siam, and *via* the Straits of Malacca to Burma and India, making short visits to Siam, Singapore, and Burma, and a longer stay in the wonderful country of the Hindus. Tibet and the Tibetans form the subject of the next chapter, and then, after travels through Persia and Arabia, the children are taken to Palestine and Turkey, and end their tour at the western terminus of the Trans-Siberian railroad, in the Ural Mountains.

The book, however, is more than an ordinary diary of travel. It pictures the Asiatic peoples as they are found in their homes, on their farms, and in their factories. It also describes in simple language the civilization of the various nations, telling how they are governed, and showing the queer features of their educational systems. The changes now going on in the various countries are pointed out, and also the influence that these changes may have upon the future of Asia in connection with us.

This book of travels is, to a large extent, the result of the original researches of the author during a two years' stay in different parts of Asia. Many of the descriptions were written on the ground, amid the scenes described, and a large part of the illustrations are from photographs taken by the author. Used as a supplement to the lessons in the text-book on geography, or for reading in connection with them, this book has also a definite and important educational purpose. By presenting to the mind's eye the various places of importance as they actually appear to a traveler, a new interest is imparted to geographical study, and what seemed before to be little more than a mere skeleton of dry facts becomes a living and potent reality.

To make the text easier to read, the pronunciation of the more difficult geographical names and foreign words is indicated, using Webster's diacritical marks.

CONTENTS.

		PAGE
I.	From America to Japan on a Big Ocean Steamer	9
II.	The Island Empire of Japan — General View	15
III.	The Wonderful City of Tokyo	24
IV.	Home Life in Japan	33
V.	The Emperor and his Palaces	43
VI.	Japanese Children at School and at Play	50
VII.	Japanese Farms and Farmers	59
VIII.	Commercial and Industrial Japan	69
IX.	The Hermit Nation	76
X.	Travels among the Koreans	85
XI.	Siberia and the Trans-Siberian Railroad	93
XII.	China — A Trip to Peking	102
XIII.	The Great Capital of China	111
XIV.	The Emperor, and how China is governed	120
XV.	The Great Wall of China	128
XVI.	Chinese Boats and the Boat People	134
XVII.	Chinese Farms and Farming	143
XVIII.	Curious Chinese Customs	154
XIX.	Siam and the Siamese	162
XX.	The King of Siam and his Royal White Elephants	170
XXI.	Singapore and the Malays	179
XXII.	Burma and the Burmese	185

		PAGE
XXIII.	Burmese Farming and the Working Elephants	194
XXIV.	General View of India	202
XXV.	Indian Farms and Farmers	209
XXVI.	The Stores and Trades of India	217
XXVII.	The Wild Animals of India	225
XXVIII.	Benares, the Holy City of the Hindus	234
XXIX.	The Native States of India; or, a Visit to the Rajah of Jaipur	241
XXX.	Above the Clouds; or, Nature and Man in the Heart of the Himalaya Mountains	249
XXXI.	Tibet and the Tibetans	257
XXXII.	Persia and the Persians	265
XXXIII.	Arabia, or Life in the Desert	273
XXXIV.	Palestine and its People	282
XXXV.	Travels among the Turks	290
XXXVI.	Russia in West Asia	297

LIST OF MAPS.

Asia	*Frontispiece*
Japan and Korea	15
Chinese Empire	103
India and Indo-China	202
Persia, Afghanistan, and Baluchistan	265
Arabia and Turkey in Asia	275
Palestine	286
Russia in Asia	301

ASIA.

I. FROM AMERICA TO JAPAN ON A BIG OCEAN STEAMER.

ASIA is the largest grand division of the globe. It is larger than North and South America, and both Europe and Africa could be spread out upon it and leave room enough around the edges for half the States of the Union. This vast area contains more than half the world's population.

Let us stop for a moment and think what that means. If all the men, women, and children on this big, round earth could be gathered together in one field, more room would be needed for the people from Asia than for all the rest; and one third of the great crowd would be of the Mongolian race, having yellow skins, and eyes which are slanting, and which when open are of the shape of an almond.

More than one fourth of the whole number would be yellow-skinned, slant-eyed Chinese, the boys and men having their heads shaved up to the crown, and long braids of black hair hanging down from their scalp locks. There would be millions of gayly dressed, almond-eyed

Chinese women, with small feet so tied up that they could not move without pain. There would be millions of Japanese mothers with little yellow babies tied to their backs, and millions of dark-faced men and women from India with features like ours. There would be yellow-skinned, slant-eyed men from Siam and Japan, with short black hair standing out over their heads like the bristles of a shoe brush; and, moving in and out through the crowd, we should see here and there a yellow-skinned Korean with his long hair done up in a knot on the crown of his head, and with a gown covering his body from his neck to his feet. There would be beautiful maidens from Burma with plugs in their ears as big round as your thumb, and women from India with rings on their fingers and bells on their toes. There would be Persians, Jews, Syrians, Armenians, and Turks, each wearing a different costume, but having many things in common with the remainder of the curious people from this Asiatic continent.

If we watched these people from Asia we should find that they do few things as we do. We should see that the men of some nations squat on their heels instead of sitting upon chairs, and that millions upon millions use wooden pillows and sleep on the floor.

If we followed them to their homes we should discover mighty cities containing hundreds of thousands of people engaged in all sorts of curious trades. We should find farms by the million, and gardens which blossom like the rose. We might visit temples and schools, and here and there we should see structures that are still the wonder of the world, such as the Great Wall of China, the gigantic bronze Buddha (bood'da) of Japan, and the Taj Mahal (täzh ma-häl') of India, the most beautiful building known to man. We should find, in short, civilizations which have much good in themselves, though they are different from ours, and we should be surprised at the wonderful but comparatively unknown world on the opposite side of the globe.

It is among these people that we are now to travel together. We shall wear for the time boots more wonderful than those of Hop-o'-my-Thumb, which enabled the little fellow to make seven leagues at a step; and we shall cross oceans and rivers, mountains and plains, stopping only to notice the most interesting sights by the way. The author will be the guide. He has traveled tens of thousands of miles through Asiatic lands, and has lived for many months among these curious peoples.

Our first trip will be across the Pacific, and we shall sail from America for the land of Japan. The Pacific is the largest of the oceans. From north to south it is more than three times as long as the distance between New York and San Francisco; and between the Western Continent and Asia, as it goes toward the south, it spreads out in the shape of a gigantic fan, forming, as it were, a great liquid wedge between our world and that on the other side of the globe. The edge of the wedge is driven in between the two great bodies of land at Bering Strait, and at this point it is only forty miles wide, a distance so short that it is said on clear days you might sit in your reindeer sledge in Alaska and see the cold hills of Siberian Russia. The wedge widens rapidly as we go to the south, and if we attempted to cross it from Quito (kē'to) along the line of the equator, we should have to travel ten thousand miles before we came to the Mo-luc'cas, a group of islands on the other side of the Pacific.

If we sailed from Lower California along the tropic of Cancer, we should have eighty-five hundred miles to go before we reached the Empire of China; and from San Francisco to Yokohä′ma, Japan, a little further north, the distance is about forty-five hundred miles. This is one of the great highroads of the Pacific, but a still shorter route can be found by going to Vancouver and taking a Canadian vessel, or by sailing on one of the American ships from Puget Sound to Japan; and this will be the road we shall travel.

"Our vessel is one of the palaces of the ocean."

Our vessel is one of the palaces of the ocean. It is propelled by steam, and the distance is now a matter of hours rather than space. It will take us from ten to twelve days to go from one continent to the other, and we feel almost as safe on the boundless Pacific as we did in our own house at home.

Our ship itself is a wonder. It is made of steel. It is nearly five hundred feet long, or long enough to stretch the whole length of the average city block; and it is so wide that it would fill a fifty-foot street. It is as high as a six-story house, and it has as many rooms as a hotel. It has its parlors and kitchens, its sleeping rooms and bathrooms, and it contains a butcher's shop, a bakery, a carpenter's shop, and all sorts of machinery. Its dining room is as large as that of a hotel, and we have as good food as on our tables at home.

Every bedroom has its electric bell, and the whole ship is lighted by electricity. Its hundreds of rooms run from story to story, from the hurricane deck, which forms its roof, down to the basement just over the keel, where a plate of steel no thicker than your finger is all that keeps out the sea. It is in this great steel shell that we travel over more than four thousand miles of water without coming in sight of land.

When we go through the workshops of the basement, the engineer shows us the great machines which, by means of steam, noiselessly but steadily force the ship on over one of the longest ocean routes in the world. He tells us that his engines are as strong as ten thousand horses, and by supposing a horse to be six feet in length from nose to tail, we find that it would take a compact line of two-horse teams more than five miles long, all pulling at once, to represent the force.

The engineer shows us the enormous amount of fuel required to feed this power, when he tells us that almost two thousand tons of coal are burned to make the steam for the voyage. It is a large dwelling house that requires ten tons of coal a year. Our steamer, therefore, in a single voyage burns enough coal to supply two hundred such homes with fuel the year round; and a village of one thousand people does not use more coal in twelve months than we shall consume in two weeks.

We find that the coal is put into the great furnaces by

thirty-two Chinamen, who are divided into gangs of eight. Each gang works for six hours at a stretch, and the shoveling goes on while we sleep; it never stops from the beginning to the end of the voyage.

We tremble when we think of the possibility of breaking down in the watery waste of the Pacific, where we might float for days and weeks without meeting another steamer.

"— the shoveling goes on while we sleep;"

We feel a little safer when the captain tells us that we are just off the Aleutian Islands, and that here the steamer sometimes sails so near land that travelers can hear the foxes bark as they go by. We feel safer still when we near the Kurile (koo'ril) Islands, and can almost smell the land of Japan. We steam on to the south, out of sight of, but not far from, the island of Yes'so, into warmer seas, and are awakened by our Chinese servant with the news that Japan is in sight, and that we shall soon be on Asiatic soil.

II. THE ISLAND EMPIRE OF JAPAN—GENERAL VIEW.

JAPAN! What a wonderful country it is! It is the Island Empire of the globe. Lying as it does, surrounded by the deep waters of the western Pacific, it winds in and out like a snake, from southwest to northeast a distance of more than two thousand miles.

This Snake is made up of more than thirty-eight hundred mountainous islands, and it drags its length through almost every climate known to man. Its tail, which is now the island of Formosa, lies in the warm waters of the semitropics, flapping, as it were, upon the tropic of Cancer. Further north, the Snake sinks the lower part of its trunk beneath the waters of the Japanese ocean current, a green

Japan and Korea.

island speck showing out here and there, and then rears it up for eleven hundred miles in the islands of Kiushu (kyoo-shoo'), Shikoku (she-kō'koo), and Hon'do, through every gradation of the temperate zone.

Its gigantic head is the island of Yesso, which lies in the cold waters of the northern Pacific, shrouded in snow during the long winter months, and at times bedded in ice. The main part of the trunk is warmed by the ocean winds to such an extent that these thousands of islands breathe an air full of moisture, and even in winter much of the land is emerald green. Now and then the snow falls on the northern part of the island of Hondo, but the green grass shows out through the white, and in many parts of Japan the plum trees are in blossom in the midst of our winter.

Japan is a land of forests and flowers. The camellia and magnolia grow wild upon its green hills, and its people call their country the land of the chrysanthemum. They cultivate the cherry tree for its blossoms, and during the season of its bloom they have picnics, when young men and maidens, old men and old women, wander about through the trees, and, inspired by the sight, write verses of poetry which they tie to the branches.

There is no land in the world which has a greater variety of beautiful scenery. It is a country of mountains and valleys, which are clothed with verdure to such an extent that you can hardly believe that the whole of Japan was once covered with volcanoes.

As we float toward the coast on our big ocean steamer, the sight that first meets our eyes is a great white mountain cone hanging almost like a silver cloud in the western horizon. As we come nearer, this cone increases in size. A long, hazy blue line of coast shows out below it through a thin veil of fleecy clouds, and we learn that we are looking at Fusiyama (foo-zĭ-ä′mä), the extinct volcano and the famed sacred mountain of Japan. It is the highest mountain of the empire, and its snowy cap kisses the sky more than two miles above us.

its snowy cap kisses the sky

As we come nearer still, we see vapor rising from another volcano on an island further off to the south; and we shall travel in and out among volcanic islands, no matter to what part of the empire we sail. Japan has to-day more than fifty steaming volcanoes, and there are hundreds of others which may at any time burst into eruption, though they now lie entirely quiet, like other mountains.

Japan is also a land of earthquakes, and its capital, To'kyo, is said to feel at least one shock every day of the year. In the past, the Japanese believed that earthquakes were caused by a gigantic fish which lived in the sea off Japan, and now and then bumped its nose or struck its tail against the coast in its anger. This it was, they thought, that shook the earth and made it crack and tremble.

" — shook the earth and made it crack — "

To-day, the scientists of Japan make careful observations of earthquakes. The government has an earthquake professor in the Imperial University, and we can learn more about them here, perhaps, than anywhere else in the world.

It will not be strange if we meet with an earthquake during our tour. One happened nearly two centuries ago which destroyed the capital (then called Yeddo), and in which two hundred thousand people lost their lives. The same city had another terrible earthquake in 1855, during which sixteen thousand houses were thrown down and many thousand persons were killed; and in 1894 the author narrowly escaped death in a great earthquake there. At this time the ground rose and fell like the waves of the sea. Some of the buildings in the palace grounds were thrown down. The home of the United States minister was almost wrecked, and several foreign buildings were entirely destroyed.

The most of these volcanic islands of Japan are small, some being no larger than a good-sized farm. Taken together, though, they form enough territory for a mighty nation, and some single islands are larger than many of our American States. The total area of Japan is greater than that of Italy, or of Great Britain and Ireland. Three States as large as New York, if they could be cut into patches like a quilt, would not be sufficient to cover it; and if you could carry the islands to Prussia, they would hide that great German kingdom from the light of the sun.

The five largest islands make up by far the most of Japan. There is Formosa at the tail of the chain, at the south, just about twice as big as New Jersey, and Yesso at the head, at the north, which is about equal to South Carolina in size. Just south of Yesso is the island of Hondo, which is larger than Kansas, and which, with its two smaller sisters, Kiushu and Shikoku, forms the most important part of Japan, taking up two thirds of its area.

As to Formosa and Yesso, these are to the rest of the empire as our unsettled territories are to the most populous States of the Union. Formosa, which was gained by war from China, is peopled by savages, some of whom, probably, are cannibals, and of whom little is known.

Yesso may be called the Alaska of Japan. It is rugged and wild, and, though it contains about one fifth of all the Japanese territory, its people are few and they are hardly more advanced in civilization than the Eskimos. They are known as the Ainos (i'nōz), and are supposed by some to have been the first Japanese. They are short in stature, like the men of the other parts of the empire, but

"The Ainos live in rude huts —"

their shoulders are broader. They are governed by the Emperor of Japan, but they have little in common with the people of the great islands to the southward.

The Ainos live in rude huts, and their bodies are so covered with hair that the people of southern Japan have nicknamed them "the hairy men." They are intemperate and as dirty as the people of the other Japanese islands are clean, and their religion is made up partly of the worship of bears.

In Hondo live the great majority of the forty millions who make up Japan's population, and upon it have been located all the great scenes of Japanese history. This is the island of which Marco Polo wrote when he returned from China, bringing his stories of Cipango, the land off the coast of Asia which was loaded with gold; and it was this island that Christopher Columbus hoped to reach first when he started out on his new route to China and discovered America. We shall look in vain for Japanese gold, though Marco Polo said that the very dogs of the country wore golden collars, and that "the roofs and floors of the ruler's palace were entirely of gold, the latter being made in plates like slabs of stone, a good two-fingers thick."

Japan has not much gold, but there are vast deposits of copper on the island of Hondo. There are iron mines and silver mines, and vast quantities of coal. We shall find coal mines in the west which run under the sea, and on the island of Takashi'ma, near Nagasä'ki, we may visit a coal mine which is now being worked, containing fifty miles of tunnels, all under the ocean.

It is on this island of Hondo that we land at the close of our voyage. We float through the picturesque Bay of Yeddo, and on into the beautiful harbor of Yokohama, where we cast our anchor amid boats from all parts of the world. There are steamers from China, and great ships which have made the voyage from London to Japan by way of the Suez Canal. There are Russian and French men-of-war, and queer-looking sailing vessels, called junks, from different parts of Japan. There are curious small boats called sampans darting out and in among the ships, each sculled by means of a paddle at the stern by a half-naked, brown-skinned, slant-eyed man who jabbers and yells as he motions to us to jump in and ride to the shore.

It is but a few minutes' trip from the ship to the wharves, and we are soon at the customhouse, where Japanese clerks in clothes like ours examine our baggage for opium and goods to be taxed. The Japanese have never allowed opium to come into their country. They have seen how the habits of opium eating and opium smoking, which are as bad in their effects as the drinking of whisky, have fastened themselves upon the Chinese, and any one who sells this drug in Japan will be dragged off to prison.

"— other jinrikishas dart by us —"

Our first sight after leaving the customhouse is a crowd of jin rik'isha men waiting to be hired. Each wears a stiff round hat covered with blue or white cotton, of the size and shape of a butter bowl upside down; and the remainder of his costume is a loose-fitting shirt and a pair of tights. Each man stands by his jinrikisha and motions to us to get in, pointing to his legs as he does so, as much as to say that he can go very fast.

As we look, other jinrikishas dart by us, filled with Japanese ladies and gentlemen, and we find that the jinrikisha is the cab of Japan. It is like an old-fashioned baby carriage, with a pair of shafts just wide enough for a man to stand between them, and with two wheels as large as those at the front end of an American buggy. It is usually pulled by one man, though sometimes by two. Some of the best runners can drag the jinrikisha from five to eight miles an hour, and many travel almost as fast as a horse. We pay only ten cents an hour for our human steeds.

It is in jinrikishas that we explore Yokohama. This is now a city of one hundred and fifty thousand people, and is the chief seaport of Japan; but it was only a fishing village when Commodore M. C. Perry landed here in 1854 and made the treaty between Japan and the United States which opened this empire to the world. Before that time, the Japanese would not have anything to do with foreigners. They knew very little about us and our civilization, and they were much surprised at the presents which Commodore Perry brought with him from America for the emperor.

Among these gifts were some telegraphic instruments and a toy railroad train. The Japanese had never seen such things, and when they learned that the telegraph wires could carry messages in Japanese quite as readily as in English, they were greatly surprised. The railroad train had a little steam engine which hauled cars so small that the Japanese could not get inside of them. They were really hardly large enough to have held children of six years. A circular track was put up at Yokohama, and the little train was run around this, many of the dignified Japanese crawling on the tops of the cars and holding on to the roof as the engine carried them flying around the track.

In our ride through Yokohama we now see many foreigners. There are telegraph wires running through its main streets. There are both electric and steam railroads connecting it with other parts of the country, and we see that the business portions of the city have many foreign stores containing goods much like those which are sold in America. We are told, however, that Yokohama is not altogether like the other towns of Japan, and we leave at once for the city of Tokyo, the capital, which is only fourteen miles off up the bay.

III. THE WONDERFUL CITY OF TOKYO.

IT is less than an hour's ride by train from Yokohama to Tokyo. The railroad skirts the beautiful Bay of Yeddo. We are carried through green rice fields, past villages of thatched houses, and are landed at last in one of the busiest parts of the capital of the Japanese Empire. Outside the station there are jinrikishas by hundreds, with their owners standing beside them. We pick out the best-looking runners, and, after a few moments' bargaining as to the price per hour we shall pay, we begin our ride through the streets.

We direct our men to carry us all over the city, and ask how long it will take to visit its principal parts. We learn that such a ride would consume several days. Tokyo is one of the largest cities of the world, for it contains a million and a half of people. It is nine miles long and eight miles in width, and its area is more than seventy square miles.

Here and there over the city are towers made of wood which rise high above the other buildings, and upon which watchmen stand day and night on the lookout for fires. One of these is not far from the railroad station. We climb to its top and take a look over the city.

Tokyo lies in a plain or wide valley which is backed by

Scene in Tokyo, Japan.

"— take a look over the city."

green hills, and cut up by canals. On the south side is the beautiful Bay of Yeddo, upon which boats of all kinds float to and fro. Running north from the bay are thousands of one- and two-story houses roofed with black tiles; and such buildings form the greater part of the city. The houses are built along the edges of streets that have no sidewalks. They are of unpainted wood turned gray by the weather, and, with their roofs, they wall the streets with long lines of black and gray. A wide river flows through the city, and upon it float queer Japanese boats. Here and there among the houses may be seen parks and gardens, in which are massive wooden buildings surrounded by trees. These are the temples where the Japanese come to worship according to their religion, of which we shall learn more farther on.

In the center of the city there is a large open space surrounded by three wide moats, or great ditches, walled with stone. These moats are filled with water. They run one inside of another, with wide spaces between them, and inclose the great park in which are the palaces of the emperor. In the grounds between the two outside moats there are some fine modern structures of brick and stone, not unlike the large public buildings of our American

"These moats are filled with water."

cities. These buildings are occupied by the great departments, through the officials of which the empire is governed.

Let us take our jinrikishas and ride through the streets. How queer it all is! The buildings look more like the bazaars of a fair than the substantial blocks of an American city. There are few large houses, and a building rarely has more than two stories. The low, ridged roofs extend about three feet beyond the walls of the houses. The floors are well up off the ground. The outer walls are made in sections which slide in grooves back and forth; and during the day the front of each lower story is pushed aside so that the passer-by can see all that goes on within. We look in vain for windows and doors. The rooms are separated from one another by walls of latticework backed with white paper, through which the light

A Japanese Store.

comes. These walls are also in sections which move aside in grooves, one inside the other; and in going from one room to another you push aside a section of the wall instead of opening a door.

The Japanese are naturally modest, but their customs are different from ours, and we see much of their family life as we ride through the streets. Here is a slant-eyed maiden making her toilet. She sits on her heels on the floor before a little round mirror, and primps, and powders, and paints her lips red, while the people go by without noticing anything strange in the scene. Next door there is a family eating their dinner. They sit or kneel on the floor, and each has his own table, of the size and height of a shoeblack's box.

Further on is a store. The merchant sits flat on the floor with his goods piled around him, and the floor is his counter. His customers sit on the floor as they shop, and he takes down piece by piece while they wait. As we look, the sections of the wall at the back are pushed wide apart, and the merchant's whole family come in to watch the sale. The little boys have almond eyes and short hair, and the little girls slant eyes and long hair done up just like their mother's. During the shopping, the merchant's bookkeeper sits on his heels at one side, and figures up the profit and loss with a box of wooden buttons strung upon wires. By moving these up and down, he adds and subtracts quite as quickly as we do with pencil and paper, and his figures rarely go wrong.

"— figures up the profit —"

But let us turn from the shops to the people. The streets of Tokyo are not narrow, and we are not jostled as we move through the crowd. The hundreds of queer-looking men and women who pass us are all good-natured, and they treat us as brothers. They smile and bend low as they meet one another, and when we stop at their stores or enter their houses, they bow again and again until we think they will break in two. We try to be polite in return, but the Japanese back is more elastic than ours. We soon grow stiff with the unusual motion, and we feel that even the India-rubber man of the circus would wear himself out with bowing in a tour through Japan.

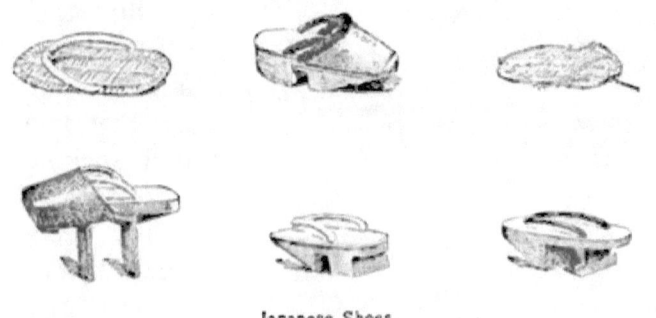

Japanese Shoes.

Clatter, clatter, clatter! What a noise the people make as they go along the street! They wear curious sandals of wood or straw, and their stockings are a kind of foot-mittens, in which the big toe has a separate place. During wet weather they wear sandals with blocks or legs on the bottom about three inches long, and the whole Japanese nation becomes just three inches taller whenever it rains. At such times the women pull their gowns up to their knees, and the men tuck theirs up under their belts, to keep them from being spattered with mud. They all carry paper umbrellas, which cover the upper parts of their bodies, and the street seems to be filled with bare yellow legs which are walking off with the people.

The Japanese dress is peculiar. Both men and women wear long, flowing gowns extending from their necks to their feet. These are folded across the body in front, and are fastened at the waist with a sash. The chief difference in the dress of women and men is in the sash, which, for the women, is usually a strip of fine silk more than half a yard wide, and so long that it can be tied in a great bow at the back. The gowns of both sexes are open at the neck.

Girls in Summer Dress.

Girls are taught in walking to take short steps and to turn their toes inward, thus becoming pigeon-toed, as it were, in order that they may not pull their dresses apart. The sleeves form the pockets, being made long and full and sewed up at the wrists. The colors of the clothes are modest in the extreme, and in our ride through the city we see silks and cottons of dark blue and gray, rather than the bright, gaudy hues which many people suppose to be most liked in Japan.

How busy every one is! As we go through the principal streets we find the stores and houses filled with workers. There are crowds at the shops buying goods, and peddlers by hundreds carrying their wares through the streets. There are porters by scores with great loads on their backs, and servants carrying heavy baskets fastened by strings or ropes to the ends of poles which rest on their shoulders.

Children in groups play about everywhere. There are whole families on their way to the theaters, which here give their performances during the day; and other families are starting out to worship at the Japanese temples, carrying a lunch in order that they may picnic in the groves after their prayers. There are Japanese

Porter with Lumber.

students walking along arm in arm, discussing their lessons. Jinrikishas pass by us, carrying Japanese statesmen to the Houses of Parliament, and other jinrikishas are seen here and there, in which are bareheaded ladies who are going out calling, or taking the air.

There are hardly any horses, and very few carriages other than jinrikishas, and as we look we are impressed with the fact that man power still runs the land of Japan. Here comes a little post-office wagon carrying the mail. It is pulled by a man who wears a blue jacket and tights. Behind is a dray of one of the big wholesale establishments, with a load of goods for the train. Its motive power consists of those two almond-eyed men who are harnessed in front, and the two others who shove hard behind with both head and hands. Their muscles stand out like thick cords as they work, and the sweat rolls down their brown skins in diamond-white streams.

We notice that most of the streets are still watered by hand, but everywhere amid these old Japanese methods of work we see that our civilization is pushing its way. Along some of the main streets there are now street cars. There are telegraph lines running through all parts of the city, and our guide points out a building which he says is the central telephone station. We find that some parts of Tokyo are lighted at night by electricity. We are told that the city has excellent public schools and a great university. We meet newsboys on every street corner, and we wonder at the changes which have taken place in Japan since the days of Commodore Perry.

"— with a load of goods for the train."

Then Tokyo was known to the world as Yeddo. It was the place where the sho'gun or tycoon' had his headquarters, and it was rather a great military camp than a city. The shogun was the commander in chief of the army. The country was then divided up into large estates owned by daimios (dī'mī-ōz), who had many soldiers. These soldiers were called sam'urai, and each of them carried two swords. They despised the tradesmen, mechanics, and farmers who made up the rest of the people, and they forced everybody to pay taxes to the daimios.

Each daimio spent a part of the year at Yeddo, living there with his soldiers, ready to march forth to war at the command of the shogun. At this time, the emperor was kept by the shogun and the daimios in the palaces at his capital, which was then the city of Kio'to, in central Japan. They pretended that he was too holy to rule, and so the shogun, daimios, and samurai governed Japan, oppressing the other classes of the people.

In 1868, however, a number of the great men of Japan decided that this must be changed. They resolved to overthrow the shogun, and to make the emperor the real ruler of the Japanese people. They began a great revolution, defeated the shogun, and brought the emperor from Kioto to Tokyo, which they made the capital of the empire. Shortly after this, Western methods of government began to be brought in. The daimios gave up their estates, receiving pay for them from the emperor, and the lands were divided among the people. All men now have equal rights, and we find that Tokyo has all the modern improvements of a city like New York or London. It has doubled in size since 1868, having since then increased in population from 700,000 to about 1,500,000.

IV. HOME LIFE IN JAPAN.

THE best place to study a people is in their own homes, and we can learn much by spending a night in a Japanese house. The Japanese live very simply, and,

"— a type of the homes of Japan."

though there is some difference between the rich and the poor, the mode of living is everywhere of the same general character, and the home of the well-to-do family which we shall visit to-day will serve as a type of the homes of Japan. We take our jinrikishas and soon reach our friend's dwelling. It is an unpainted frame building of two stories, with a heavy roof of black earthenware tiles supported by gray wooden posts which rest upon stones. We can see clear through the house and get a glimpse of a beautiful garden lying behind. The outer walls have been pushed back for the day, for the sun is warm; and the air rushes through on all sides.

We see almost the whole house before we leave our jinrikishas, and as we look we wonder at first if the family has not moved away. The rooms are all here, but there

"The rooms are all here"

is nothing like our American furniture in sight. Where are the tables? There are none, for the Japanese do not use such tables as ours. Where are the chairs? Those cushions which lie on the mats take their places, for these people prefer to sit on the floor.

How clean everything is! The road in front of the house is well swept. You can see yourself in the strip of bare floor which runs round the house about two feet above the ground, like a porch; and the rooms just back of this are covered with matting of the cleanest white straw. This matting forms the carpet of Japan. It is not made like that which is sent to America. It is woven in mats three feet wide, six feet long, and about twice as thick as this book. These are bound at the edges with black cloth, and they are fitted together closely, so that the floor is covered with panels of white bordered with black. The mats are of the same size all over Japan, and the size of a room is known, not as so many feet wide and so many feet long, but by the number of mats required to cover the floor.

How is the house heated? There are no stoves in sight, and there is no cellar or basement in which a furnace might be hidden. The house has no chimney, and there are no signs of stovepipes. The heating is done by little brass-lined boxes filled with ashes, in the center of which a handful of charcoal is burning. These boxes are known as hibachis (hī-bä -chēz). They are common all over Japan. They form a poor means of heating during cold weather, and, as winter comes on, the people keep warm by putting on more underclothing, so that the nation appears to be growing fatter and fatter as the weather grows colder. But how can they cook without stoves? They have little clay ovens in which they put charcoal, and boil and fry over the coals.

Hibachi.

Let us go into the house. As we approach, a little maidservant comes to the front. She gets down on her knees, spreads out her hands on the floor, and bumps her little head on the mats in order to show us respect. She asks us to take off our shoes and come in. The Japanese never wear shoes in the house, and we have already learned that it would be far more polite to keep our hats on than our shoes. So in our stocking feet we step up into the house, and take our seats on the cushions.

HOME LIFE.

Very soon some of the family come in. They bow low, getting down on their knees and bending again and again to the floor. As they rise, they suck in their breath with a loud, half-whistling sigh, as though they were overcome by the honor which we are conferring upon them by calling. We do the same as we bow in return. Then the maidservant brings in a little box of charcoal for lighting our pipes, for in Japan every one is expected to smoke. She next fetches a little tray which she places before us on the floor. It contains a porcelain teapot and some little cups, each about the size of half an eggshell. The little servant gets down on her knees and offers them to us, with a bow. We drink from them in Japanese style, sucking the tea in with a loud sipping noise to show that we like it.

Here come the children who have been playing in the garden back of the house. They are dressed like their parents, and they bow to us in the same way. They are very respectful, for to have a bad child in Japan is disgraceful, and all Japanese children honor their parents.

" — a porcelain teapot

The mother takes one of the little boys in her arms, and rubs her cheeks against his. It is in this way that the Japanese show their affection. They do not kiss, nor do they shake hands, though boy friends and girl friends often go about with their arms around one another's shoulders or waist, and the members of a family show that they are fond of each other.

What is that on this little one's back?

That is a doll, and the little girl is carrying her baby. The mothers here often go about with their babies tied to their backs, and the children sometimes do the same with their dolls. As soon as a girl is old enough, she is taught to take care of her little sister in this way, and as we ride through the streets we shall see children with live babies hung to their shoulders. A girl of eight or nine years sometimes has a little baby tied to her back, and carries it about as she plays. The baby blinks out of its queer eyes at the great world around it, and when it grows tired it drops its head on its shoulder and sleeps away while the little girl nurse goes on making mud pies, or playing with a ball, or at other games.

'— when it grows tired —"

Our Japanese friends invite us to take supper with them and to stay over night. They entertain us in the parlors, which, as is often the case in Japan, are at the back of the house. Soon they tell us that the bath is prepared, and as the honored guests we have the first turn.

The Japanese are exceedingly cleanly, and every well-to-do home has its own bathroom. It is a sign of good breeding to ask a guest to have his bath first. The custom is such that all the family, no matter how many the children, bathe in the same water and in the same tub, and the servants get in at the last. No soap is used until after getting out of the tub, and the body is finally washed off by pouring water over it with a basin after the soaping. There are public baths in all the cities, and in Tokyo they number eight hundred, in which three hundred thousand people bathe daily at a cost of less than one cent for each person, so that even the poorest can keep themselves clean.

HOME LIFE.

The little maidservant comes and leads us to the bathroom. It is a clean little room with movable walls of white pine. She pulls one section of the walls back, and we enter. In one corner of the room a stream of cold water flows through a wooden pipe into a barrel, from which a trough carries it off into a little brook that flows through the garden outside. From this barrel we shall get cold water after we are through with our bath, and with that shining brass basin which we see on the floor we can pour cold or warm water over our bodies after using the soap.

The bath tub is of wood. It is much like a short, oval barrel. It has a charcoal fire under it, with a stovepipe running up through the water at the back of the tub, this pipe being protected by a strip of white pine which keeps one's body from touching it. As we look, the water smokes slightly, but it seems no warmer than milk when fresh from the cow; and, having undressed, we jump in. Whew! How hot it is! The water is almost boiling, and we gasp as we sink, half scalded, to the bottom. We climb out very quickly, finding our skins now as red as a beet, and the little servant, who stands outside the wall and peeps in, giggles as she enters and hands us our clothes. The Japanese are fond of hot baths, and the people of all ages, from grandparents to babies, take them every day.

" — not quite a foot high "

By this time supper is ready, and we shall have a Japanese meal. We all eat together, but each has his own table. It is not quite a foot high, and we sit on the floor as we eat. The first course is Japanese wine or sä-ke with sweet cake and candy. This is brought in by our

Japanese Family at Dinner

little maidservant, who gets down on her knees and bows low as she hands it to us. Next comes a soup made of beans, and with it raw fish cut in slices and served with a queer sauce called soy. This is of a dark brown color, and is made of a mixture of vinegar, salt, and fermented wheat. Then there are salads and pickles of various kinds. There are green pears as hard as stones, so served because the Japanese like this fruit green.

"The rice is brought in—"

The supper closes with rice and tea. The rice is brought in to us in a big, round, wooden box of the shape and size of a peck measure. It is offered to us again and again, for the theory is that no one need go away hungry if he has plenty of rice. The tea is served in little cups, but we notice that our Japanese friends sometimes pour their tea into their rice.

Throughout the meal we watch our friends eat, and as far as possible act like them. The soup is offered to us in bowls, the size of a large coffee cup. Each of us has a bowl, and we drink the soup by raising it to our lips. The fish, rice, and salads we try to eat with our chopsticks, but this we find very hard to do. If you will take two slate pencils, balance them between the two first fingers and the thumb of your right hand, and try to pick up grains of rice and bits of hash with their ends, you can see with what difficulty the first Japanese meal is eaten.

Hand with Chopsticks.

Even well-to-do people of Japan seldom have more than two courses at a meal. They eat three meals a day, — a breakfast on rising, a dinner at noon, and another meal at sunset. The eggs and fowl on their tables are well prepared. The Japanese make delicious fish soups, and they broil and fry fish, making dishes fit for a king. They eat but little meat, and they do not have butter or cheese. Rice forms the chief part of the food eaten by most of the people, but some are so poor that they cannot afford rice, and millet, a kind of grass seed, and other grains are used in its stead.

The supper over, the family sit around on the floor and chat. The neighbors come in, and all, both women and men, smoke little pipes as they talk. The children play games. Those who are in school perhaps study their lessons for the morrow, and the little girls play with their dolls. And so our evening passes until the time comes for sleep. Then there is a commotion. The servants go out to shut up for the night. They pull the sliding walls to, until the whole house becomes a well-closed box, and the only ventilation is through the cracks at the corners.

Japanese Bed.

We have been wondering all the time where we should sleep. We have gone through the house, and so far have seen no sign of a bed. Our little maidservant takes us upstairs. She slides back a board which hides a recess in the wall, and pulls out armful after armful of soft, thick quilts or comforts. She lays these on the floor, one on top of another, and turns down the last one for a cover. We look for the sheets, and are told that the Japanese do not use them. Then we ask for pillows, and the maid gives each of us a block of wood about the size of a brick. This stands on its side, and has a roll of soft paper on top. We are expected to put them under our necks, and let our heads hang over the edges while we sleep. We try it, but find that, though they do for Japan, they will not do for America; so we roll up our coats and use them instead, and are soon dreaming of home.

"— the size of a brick"

V. THE EMPEROR AND HIS PALACES.

WE shall visit to-day some of the high officials of Japan, and shall learn something of how the empire is governed. The emperor rules through his cabinet and parliament, and our first journey will be to his majesty's palaces. He has a vast estate in the heart of Tokyo, made up of hill and valley, and containing lakes and woods and several acres of one-story palaces. The grounds, as we have seen, are surrounded by wide moats, and upon the water magnificent lotus flowers float on their green leaves. We cross the moats on bridges of marble, and, passing soldiers and servants in European clothes, find ourselves in the home of the Japanese ruler.

The palaces are of wood, built much after the style of the Japanese temples, of which we shall learn later on. They have hundreds of rooms, and many of the walls consist of sliding screens of plate glass, which move in grooves and can be pushed back so that many rooms can be thrown into one. Some of the ceilings are decorated with the finest embroideries, and one room is ceiled with woven gold tapestry that cost ten thousand dollars. The walls of the other rooms are covered with brocaded silks as fine as that of a ball dress, and the inlaid floors have matting almost as soft as a velvet carpet.

There are all sorts of flowers in the emperor's gardens, and his lakes are filled with many kinds of fish. He has large ponds, fed by canals, where he takes part with his nobles in the netting of ducks. This is a favorite amusement of the rich Japanese. There are many wild ducks about Tokyo, and, as they fly over the palace grounds, they are enticed to alight by means of decoy-ducks which float on the emperor's ponds. Other decoys are scattered along the little canals which run out from the ponds, and which are so lined with trees and bushes that a man can easily hide on their banks. Grain is scattered about in the canals as bait, and when the ducks swim after this, the emperor and his nobles, concealed in the bushes, catch them by throwing nets over their heads. It requires great skill to throw a net properly, and the princes are said to delight in the sport.

You must not think, however, that duck netting is the chief business of the Japanese ruler. He is a hard-working monarch, and most of his time is occupied in managing the government of his country. His cabinet ministers bring him daily reports from all parts of his empire, and he has the American newspapers translated, so that he can tell what they are saying about Japan.

The emperor's quarters in the palace are entirely separate and apart from those of the empress. Her majesty has a complete court of her own, with her secretaries and servants. She is at the head of all movements for the advancement of Japanese women. Like his majesty, the empress now wears foreign clothes upon state occasions. She has abandoned the old Japanese custom whereby a wife shaved off her eyebrows and blackened her teeth in order to show her devotion to her husband by making herself so ugly that it would be impossible for any one else to admire her. This horrible fashion, however, has prevailed widely in Japan until lately, and, as we shall see, it still exists in some parts of the country.

"They tie their prisoners —

We pass many policemen on our way back from the palace, and see that good order is everywhere kept. The police dress in clothing much like that which we wear, but they all carry swords. They tie their prisoners with ropes, and drive or drag them on the way to the jail. Japan has now as good a police system as ours, and there are police stations scattered all over the empire. There are many detectives, and the spy system of the Emperor of Japan is almost as efficient as that of the Czar of Russia.

In making our tour through the country, we learn that we must have passports, or papers showing just who we are and where we are going. Each passport must contain the name of the owner and a full description of just how he looks. It gives his age and height, and tells whether his eyes are brown, blue, black, or gray. These papers will be asked for at every city or village we visit, and the hotel keepers must see them before they will give us our rooms. Every foreigner in the Japanese Empire must have a paper of this kind; and if he cannot show it upon the demand of the police, he is regarded as a suspicious character, and may be thrown into prison. In this way the emperor knows just who are in his country, and what they are doing, and he can tell almost to a man where every stranger sleeps every night. His own people are not allowed to leave the country without the permission of the government, and those who break the laws are almost sure to be punished.

Japan now has good courts. It has hundreds of lawyers, and every man is allowed a fair trial. The greatest penalty permitted is death by hanging, and for small offenses the fines are sometimes as low as five cents.

In the past, the laws were made by the shogun and the emperor. Now the Japanese people make laws for themselves through their Houses of Parliament. The Upper House is composed of the nobles, and the most of the members are chosen by the nobility, though some receive their appointment directly from the emperor. The members of the House of Representatives are elected by the people. Every Japanese man has to be twenty-five years old before he can vote, and a voter must have enough property so that his taxes amount to at least fifteen dollars a year.

The Houses of Parliament have officers much like our Houses of Congress. The members make speeches, and they discuss all measures relating to public affairs. They vote all the money that is to be used in carrying on the government, with the exception of the emperor's household expenses, with which they have nothing to do. The people of Japan formerly had but few rights. They were forced to pay such taxes as were demanded by the nobles

THE EMPEROR AND HIS GOVERNMENT.   47

and the army. Now they fix their own taxes, and everything is fair and just.

The parliament buildings are situated in Tokyo, not far from the palace. There is a big wall around them which is entered by gates, and when the houses are in session you see on each side of these gates about five hundred black jinrikishas, with barelegged men in butter-bowl hats,

Parliament House, Interior.

tights, and blue jackets, sitting in them, waiting for their employers, the members of parliament, to come out.

Leaving the parliament buildings, it is but a short drive to the Department of War, where the officers stay who control all matters relating to the Japanese army. The emperor has now one of the best armies of the world; every Japanese boy of seventeen years is expected to enter some branch of it, and after he becomes a man he has seven years to serve as a soldier.

The rifle used by the army was invented by a Japanese, and is one of the best in the world. The soldiers are

trained by officers, many of whom have been educated in the German army, and it was this training that enabled the little Japanese nation to conquer the great nation of China, which has about ten times as many people. Japan has a fine modern navy, and its warships are equal to those of the great nations of Europe.

We shall find that one of the most important officers of the emperor's cabinet is the minister of communications. His department has to do with the postal and telegraph systems of the empire.

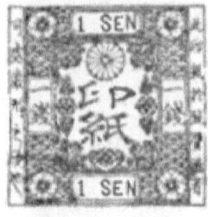

In the past, all letters in Japan were carried by messengers, whose costume consisted chiefly of a cloth about the waist, and of a rich coat of tattooing. The service was so expensive that only the rich could afford to send letters.

Now Japan has a postal system like ours, and letters are sent to all parts of the country for two cents apiece.

An American from our Post Office Department at Washington went to Japan and showed the emperor how we carried our letters, and he ordered that his officers should introduce the same methods there. The Japanese

Japanese Postage Stamps.

now make their own postage stamps. They have postal cards, and if we call at the Post Office Department, we

THE EMPEROR AND HIS GOVERNMENT.   49

can learn that the postal service in one year carried over three hundred million letters, and more than eighty million newspapers and periodicals.

We shall meet Japanese postmen on the streets of every city we visit. They wear blue clothes, and their blue-mittened feet rest on straw sandals. They deliver their letters at all the houses, and collect from the street postal boxes, just as our American postmen do. The telegraph system is equally good. All the lines belong to the government, and you can telegraph more cheaply in Japan than in America.

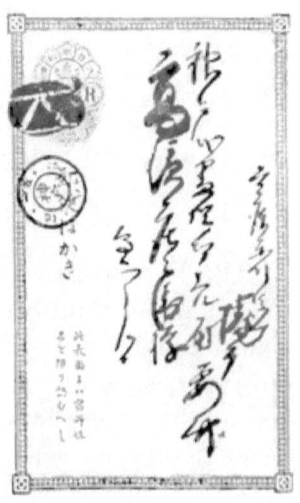

"They have postal cards —"

We visit also the Treasury Department, one division of which makes the money of Japan. The Japanese use gold, silver, copper, and paper as money. They have a banking system much like that of the United States, and in the Bureau of Engraving they make their own bank notes. The unit is the yen, which is a silver coin of the size and shape of our silver dollar. Each yen contains one hundred sen, or cents, and each sen contains ten rin. There are fifty-sen, twenty-sen, ten-sen, and five-sen pieces of silver. There are nickel coins worth five sen, and copper pieces of two sen, one sen, one half sen.

"We shall meet Japanese postmen —"

and one rin, or one tenth of a sen. The paper money is in bills of one yen, five yen, ten yen, and upwards, the bills being wider than, but not so long as, our national bank notes.

VI. JAPANESE CHILDREN AT SCHOOL AND AT PLAY.

JAPAN now has public schools, and the little yellow-skinned, slant-eyed Japanese can have an education almost equal to that of children in the United States. In the Japanese cities there are more than one hundred kindergartens, where little girls and boys of from three to six years begin their school life. All children are compelled by law to attend school from their sixth to their tenth year, and there are advanced grades for those who wish to study longer.

Many Japanese families are so poor that they need the help of their children who are more than ten years old; and such children are then put to work in the fields, in stores, at trades, or in the factories. Thousands of boys, however, are kept at school until they are grown up, having most of the studies taught in our country. Hundreds attend the colleges which are to be found in the different Japanese cities, and many graduate yearly at the Imperial University at Tokyo.

The empress has established a girls' school at the capital, where the daughters of princes and nobles are educated. Here they study French, German, and English, and learn everything fitted to make them good wives for the men who are to govern Japan when they are grown up.

The studies of Japanese children are more difficult than

ours. We have only twenty-six letters in our alphabet. The Japanese have forty-seven in theirs, and there are so many word signs in addition that an educated man must know thousands of characters. Many of the signs mean whole words or short sentences, and there are curious endings and crooks which have to be learned.

Let us visit a primary school, — not one of the new city schools, some of which now have desks like our own, but one of the common primary schools, such as we shall find all over the country. It is early in the morning, and the children, dressed in gowns, stand about with their books in little satchels hung from their backs.

Here comes the teacher. We can hear him afar off, as he clatters along on his wooden sandals. He wears a gown of dark gray, and has spectacles covering his eyes. As he approaches, the children bow down almost to their knees, and as they rise they suck in their breath as a polite mark of respect. The teacher does likewise, and he smiles upon them as he comes up to the house, and, placing his sandals on the ground, walks over the white mats on the floor of the schoolroom and takes his seat under the blackboard. He may have a chair, or he may sit on the floor with a low desk before him.

The scholars as they come in leave their sandals in order outside. They squat in their stocking feet on the floor mats, and study with their books on their knees.

How queer the books are! They begin at the back instead of the front, and the lines run up and down the page instead of across it. What curious letters! They remind us of the Chinese characters which we see on the tea boxes, and they seem almost alike.

Here is a class of five boys learning their letters. The teacher makes the characters on the blackboard, and the boys copy them on sheets of paper, singing out their names as they do so. Do they write with pencils or pens? No, they have brushes much like those we use for water colors, and they paint the letters with black India ink. Notice how they hold the brush as they write. Their hands do not touch the paper, the brush is almost vertical, and instead of writing, as we do, across the page from left to right, they begin on the right hand of the sheet, and paint their lines from the top to the bottom. Each child has an ink stone beside him. Upon this he puts a few drops of water, and then rubs the stone with a little black cake of India ink, thus making his own ink as he writes. No blotters are needed. The paper is soft and porous, and sucks in the ink as it comes from the brush.

A Writing Lesson.

There is a little boy learning to count with the sorobän, an aid to calculation by which the Japanese, to a large extent, dispense with mental arithmetic. It is a box of wooden buttons strung upon wires, as wide as this book and about a foot long, like the one we saw the bookkeeper use in the store. The buttons represent units, tens, hundreds, thousands, etc., and by moving them up and down, the Japanese boy is

The Soroban.

able to do sums of addition, subtraction, multiplication, and division; and it is said that any sum in arithmetic can be done in this way upon the soroban, even to extracting square and cube root.

In some of the schools we shall find translations of American text-books, and many of the scholars will tell us that they think their hardest study is English, because everything connected with it seems to go wrong end foremost. They must begin at what seems to them the wrong end of the book. They write from the other side of the page, and the sentences seem to go across the page the wrong way. They also find the pen very awkward to handle, but they feel that they must learn to write English, for the government officials and the best business men of Japan now understand this language and use it.

In the past, the boys of the upper classes looked forward to the day when they could go about wearing two swords, and when their chief business would be fighting. Now "the pen is mightier than the sword," for Japan has become a land of books and newspapers. It has large bookstores and great printing establishments. There are now published thirty-five Japanese magazines devoted to law. There are scores of different papers treating of farming. There are all kinds of scientific journals, and daily newspapers are sold in all the cities. We meet many Japanese newsboys, who go about the streets, each ringing a bell as the sign that he has papers for sale.

The Japanese newspapers, like the books, begin at the back. Their columns are wider than those of our papers, and run horizontally across the page instead of up and down it. The lines run up and down the columns instead of across them, and you begin to read at the top of a line instead of at the side. You read to the bottom of the

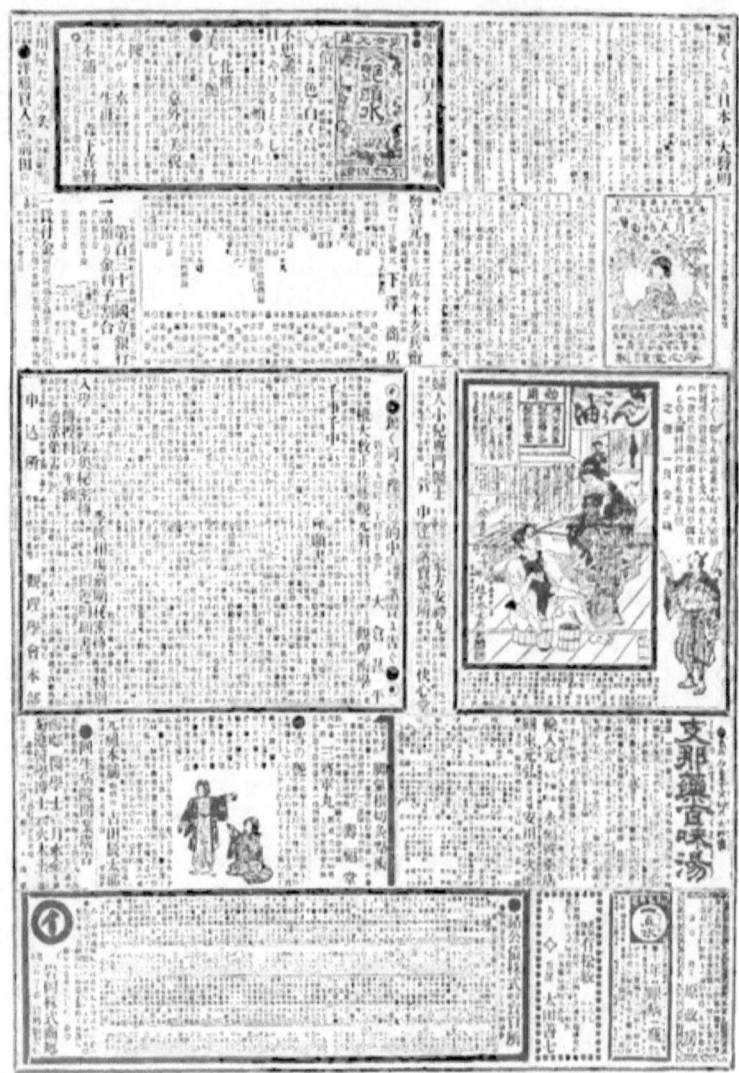

Japanese Newspaper, One Page.

first line, and then go to the top of the one next to the left, and so on until you come to the end of the sentence. This is marked by a Japanese period, which is a little circle, instead of the dot we use. The newspapers contain advertisements, editorials, and all kinds of telegraphic dispatches.

It takes a vast number of characters to form the type for one issue of a Japanese paper, and sometimes a thousand different letters may be used on the same page. The characters are so many that in a Japanese printing office a number of boys are employed to run about through the cases and collect the type for the compositors, who call out the names of the letters they want.

How about play? Are the lives of Japanese children made up of nothing but school and hard work? No, indeed; they play fully as hard as they study, and they have as much fun as any boys and girls in the world. They have all sorts of playthings, and there are toy stores in all the cities. There are peddlers who wander about through the country selling nothing but toys, and there are men who carry little ovens or stoves with real fire in them about the streets, and who have sweet dough for sale. A boy or girl can rent a stove for an hour for less than five cents, and the stove man will furnish the dough, and look on while the child makes up cakes and bakes them. Sometimes the man cuts out Japanese letters, and the child cooks them and learns their names as it plays. There are men who sit in the streets and mold animals, jinrikishas, and other things of rice paste for children, according to their orders, for a very small sum.

The dressing of dolls is a great pastime for girls. There are three days of every year during which all the people celebrate what is called the Feast of Dolls. At this time all the dolls which have been kept in the family for generations are brought forth, set upon shelves covered with red cloth, and admired. Some of them represent the emperor and the empress, and are treated with great honor, receiving the best food of the play feasts, to which the dolls are treated three times a day. After the three days are ended, these dolls are put away, but the little

"— selling nothing but toys —"

Japanese girl has other dolls with which she plays the year round.

There is also a day devoted to the boys. We shall know it by seeing great balloonlike paper fishes floating in the air from sticks fastened to the roof of each house in which a boy baby has been born during the year, and also from other houses where the parents are glad they have boys. The Japanese boys have kites of all kinds and shapes. Some are singing kites, which make a music like that of an Æolian harp as they float in the air, kept steady by two long tails, one tied to each lower corner. Others are made in the shapes of dragons and babies, eagles and butterflies, and all sorts of animals.

Some kites have their strings soaked with glue into which powdered glass is dusted, for a length of thirty feet from the kite. When the glue hardens, this part of the string becomes as sharp as a file. These are called fighting kites. The boys try to get the strings of two of them crossed while in the air, and each pulls his kite this way and that until one of the glass-powdered strings saws the other in two. In such cases the owner of the victorious kite is entitled to the one which has been cut loose.

Japanese children have games of instruction, as well as games of pure play. They have block maps made of pieces, and by putting these together they learn the shape of Japan and of the world. They have a game much like our "Authors," called "One Hundred Verses of One Hundred Poets," which teaches them the names and best sayings of the great Japanese scholars. Many of the games they play teach them lessons in morals. For instance, one of their games is like our "Pussy wants a corner;" but in Japan the "pussy" is known by a name which represents a Japanese devil, and the corners of the room are called the Harbors of Truth, in which places only can safety be found.

The Japanese have two great religions. One is called Shin'to-ism. It is the oldest religion of Japan, and consists largely of the worship of the heroes of Japanese history. The other is Buddhism, which was introduced into Japan about 600 A.D., and of which we shall learn more in Siam and India. Connected with these religions there are gods of all kinds, and many persons have their favorite gods. Every Japanese house has a little shrine in it, before which the people place offerings and pray; and there are public shrines and temples devoted to religion in all parts of Japan. Some of these are considered especially holy, and pilgrims by the thousands, with staves in their hands and with baggage tied to their backs, walk from one holy place to another to offer their prayers.

We meet Buddhist priests, who go about with shaved heads, and we spend hours in admiring the beautiful temples which have been erected to Buddha. They are one-story structures of wood, with heavy roofs of black tiles. Many of them are of vast extent, and the interiors of some are gorgeous with carvings. Some temples have rooms papered with gold leaf and walled with paintings by the Japanese masters, and many of them contain images plated with gold.

Japanese Priest.

Japan has one statue of Buddha which is among the great art works of the world. This we visit at Kamaku′ra, a small town on the seacoast not far from Yokohama. The statue is made of bronze plates so fitted together that the joints cannot be seen. It is known as the Dai Butzu (dī boot′soo). It is an immense sitting figure as tall as a four-story house. We get some idea of its size when we find that its bronze thumbs are so large that

" — as tall as a four-story house."

two men can sit on one of them and have room to spare, and that its eyes, which are of gold, are each three feet in length.

VII. JAPANESE FARMS AND FARMERS.

THE country scenes are among the most interesting sights of Japan. Let us leave Tokyo and make a tour overland to the cities in the central part of the empire. How shall we travel? We might go by railroad, and, in cars much like ours, could ride from one town to another almost as fast as on our trains at home. We should find the cars filled with Japanese people, and might note that many of the girls and boys, not used to foreign benches and chairs, squat on the cushions, with their feet tucked beneath them. Japan is fast building railroads. Great trunk lines now connect all the main centers, and the rates of fare are exceedingly low.

"— cars filled with Japanese people —"

The railroad, however, is too quick for our journey. We want to see something of Japanese farms, and to learn how the people live in the country. So we will take jinrikishas, with two men to each carriage, and will ride almost as fast as though we had horses. One man will pull in the shafts, and the other will push hard behind when we go up the hills, or by a rope will harness himself to the front and run on ahead. We soon get over our shame at driving our almond-eyed brothers, and we poke our human steeds in the back and urge them to hurry.

We find the roads very good. There are villages every few miles, and we stay at night in country hotels, where we must sleep on the floor. The landlord's children watch us with wonder as we come in. When we have gone to our rooms, they may poke their fingers through the paper walls, and, gluing their eyes to the holes, see how the

FARMS AND FARMING. 61

strange foreigners look as they take off their clothes and prepare to go to sleep. Some of them have never before seen an American, and our straight eyes and fair faces seem to them very queer.

We have some rainy days on our journey, during which we pass many travelers wearing the waterproof cloak of Japan. This is a sort of shawl of rice straw which hangs from the shoulders, and which, with the big straw hat above it, makes the wearer look like a gigantic yellow bird trotting along through the fields. We cross now and then over mountains so steep that we must leave our jinrikishas and be carried by men in conveyances known as kä-gōs. The kago is a basket-work chair hung to a long pole, which is carried on the shoulders of men. You squat in the chair crosslegged, and hold on for dear life as your men carry you along precipices, over the stones of rushing mountain streams, going up hill and down.

"— the waterproof cloak of Japan."

We pass through much beautiful scenery. Japan is made up of mountains and valleys, and the moist air keeps nature refreshingly green. The mountains feed many short rivers, and brooks by the hundreds gurgle down the green hills. The Japanese understand the science of irrigation, and some of these streams are dammed up in the mountains, and the water is carried

The Kago.

from one place to another through winding ditches, so that one stream feeds many farms. The hills are often cut into different levels or terraces, over which the streams flow successively on their way to the valleys.

The mountainous nature of Japan is such that less than one tenth of the empire is under cultivation; but that tenth gives more than half of the people constant employment, and it produces enough to feed Japan's entire population. The soil for farming is not richer than ours, but the Japanese so increase its fertility by good cultivation that one acre often produces from three to five times as much as the same space does in America; and it is said that there are farms in Japan which for centuries have produced two crops every year.

How queer the farms are! The whole country looks like a vast garden, with ponds of silvery-white water showing out through the green. There are no very large fields, the average farm being less than two acres in size. The crops are of all shades and colors, from the gold of ripe wheat to the green of sprouting rice. We look over the fields in vain for fences, houses, and barns. The

A Farmer's House.

Japanese have no fences. They do not live on their farms, but in villages of thatched wooden houses strung along the main roads. There is no need of barns, as the crops are sold almost as soon as they are harvested.

There are very few horses, cows, or sheep. In some parts of the empire the people would look upon sheep as wild animals, and a cow would be as great a curiosity as the elephant is to us. The horses we see are not bigger than good-sized ponies. They are used chiefly as pack horses, though now and then we pass one hitched to a cart and led by a big-hatted peasant.

We notice that the horses are shod with straw shoes. The straw is so braided that it forms a round mat about half an inch thick, which is fastened to the animal's foot by straw strings running around the leg just above the hoof. Each pack horse has a stock of fresh shoes tied to his saddle, and the farmer who leads him looks now and then at his feet, and changes his shoes as soon as they become worn. Such shoes cost less than one cent a set. The distances through the country districts are often measured by the number of shoes which the horses wear out while traveling them, and it is said that the average horseshoe will last for a walk of eight miles.

We find that the farmers of Japan have not been greatly affected by our civilization. They think, act, and live much as they did in the past, and we observe everywhere the customs of the old Japan. We see Japanese women whose heads are shaved close to the scalp, and who have no sign of eyebrows. They seem homely indeed, and upon inquiry we learn that they are widows who keep their heads shaved in order to show their grief for the loss of their husbands. We see many women who look very pretty until they open their mouths; but then we notice that their teeth are as black as a pair of new rubber shoes. They are farm wives who are destroying their beauty to show their husbands that they do not care for the attentions of others. The men in some cases have their heads shaved on the top, with the long locks at the side and the back fastened up on the crown of the head in a stiff queue like a door knocker. This is the old style of wearing the hair, and was the usual fashion some years ago.

The men at work in the fields wear hardly any clothes, and we see some who have on nothing except a flat hat of white straw, as big as a parasol, and a cloth tied around the waist. We see children with tools on their shoulders, on their way to the fields. We see barefooted women clad in big hats and blue cotton gowns, and notice that there are as many women as men at work out of doors. The women and men work side by side, and the children have their share in the toil. How hard

Plowing Rice Ground.

they all work! They dig up the ground with mattock and spade. There are but few plows or other modern implements, and all sorts of seeds are planted by hand. The harvesting is likewise done by hand, and we see that it is human muscle which makes Japan's bread.

The crops are of all kinds, for nearly everything can be raised in Japan. We see patches of wheat and barley, of tobacco and cotton, and of other plants which are strange to our eyes. We go through thousands of rice fields. Rice is the most important crop of the country, for it forms the chief food of the people. The majority of the world's inhabitants eat rice, and for at least one third of them it is the principal food.

There are almost as many different kinds of rice as there are different kinds of apples, and the Japanese rice is among the best. It requires great care in its cultivation. The grains must first be sowed in soil which is well soaked with water. They sprout in four or five days, and within a month or six weeks they are ready to be transplanted. The rice fields have in the mean time been flooded. The farmers now take the young sprouts, and

and set them out in the mud."

in their bare feet wade through the water and set them out in the mud. They flood the fields again and again during the summer. They keep the rice free from weeds, and by the latter part of September the crop is ready for harvest.

The rice plants grow much like our wheat or oats. At first they are a beautiful green, but as they ripen they become a bright yellow. The straw is cut close to the

FARMS AND FARMING.

ground with a sickle, and is tied up in little sheaves which are hung over a pole resting on legs, so that the heads of rice are off the ground. The grains are pulled from the stem by drawing the straw through a rack which has teeth like a saw. The grains fall off and are laid away to be husked when required. We find rice fields in all the lowlands of the island of Hondo, and in many other parts of Japan.

Cleaning Rice.

We stop now and then at the tea fields or tea gardens, which are to be found throughout the greater part of the empire; and, as we get nearer Kioto, in central Japan, we spend a few days in the region of Uji (oo'jē), where the tea grown is especially fine. One kind is known by a Japanese word meaning "jeweled dew," and is worth from five to eight dollars a pound. It is in Uji that the tea for the emperor and empress has been grown for years.

The tea plant of Japan is a kind of camellia. It grows much like the American box, and it is carefully cultivated

"— the hedges run in parallel rows —"

in hedges which rise to a height of from three to five feet, and which are usually about two feet in width. In a tea garden the hedges run in parallel rows from one side to the other, the rows being about as far apart as those of a potato field. The leaves, which form the tea of commerce, look somewhat like those of a rosebush, their color being a very bright green.

The plants produce their best tea from the fifth to the tenth year, but some plants are said to live longer than the life of a man. They are picked several times during the season, the first tea crop of each year being the best. The work is done almost entirely by girls, who walk through the bushes and pick out the bright, new, green leaves from the old, dark ones. They put the leaves in great baskets and carry them off on their backs.

Weighing Tea, Japan.

The leaves are dried in the sun, then steamed, and dried again. That part of the crop intended for export is then shipped to the tea factories at the ports, where all the moisture is taken out of the leaves by rubbing them about in great iron bowls set in ovens. This rubbing is done by the hands of women and men, and under it the leaves change their shape until they become the little, hard, twisted things that we buy as tea in America. After they are thoroughly dried, they are sorted by Japanese girls, and then packed in boxes for shipment. The work is all done by hand, and every cup of tea that we drink is made from leaves, each of which has been handled again and again by Japanese (or other Asiatic) men, women, and children.

VIII. COMMERCIAL AND INDUSTRIAL JAPAN.

RIDING through tea gardens, passing by great fields of cotton, and finding at every few miles villages busy with the making of porcelain, cotton, and silk goods, we at last come to Kioto. The region about the cities of Kioto and O'säkä is one of the busiest parts of the world. We find in Kioto men and women weaving beautiful silks on the rudest of looms, not far from modern silk mills; and in Osaka we may see large cotton mills, in which the long-stapled raw cotton, shipped by the thousands of bales from our Southern States, is mixed with the shorter Japanese cotton, and, with modern machinery, is woven into all sorts of cloths for the people.

We find many factories devoted to the manufacture of the jute rugs which are shipped to America from Japan;

and we are surprised to see that these beautiful rugs are woven in most cases by children of ten years and upwards, who receive for a day's work from five to ten cents. The women and men also get low wages; and when we enter the workingmen's homes, and note how cheap everything is, we see that the Japanese could easily live upon what we of the United States waste. We notice the introduc-

Cobbler, using Feet.

tion of our labor-saving inventions, and wonder if the time will not soon come when these people, with their great skill and low wages, will be competing with our workmen in all kinds of goods and in all the world's markets.

At present the greater part of the work is done by hand. Nearly all the native manufactures are produced in this way. In the villages given up to the making of porcelain we see numerous small factories where the clay is modeled by hand, and where the artists squat on the floor and paint the vases and dishes with the beautiful and curious designs found on Japanese china.

There are artists who carve rats and monkeys and many other figures out of ivory tusks, to be shipped as curios all over the world. There are shops in which Japanese lanterns are being made, where dozens of boys and girls squat together, bending bamboo hoops into the proper

Japanese Cooper.

shapes and pasting the paper upon them. There are umbrella makers and fan makers sitting in their shops by the roadside and drying their goods in the sun.

As we look, we see that the Japanese artisan has what is equal to four hands and twelve fingers. He is usually barefooted, and he uses his feet almost as much as his hands. He holds all sorts of articles steady by pressing them between the soles of his feet. His two great toes are equal to two extra fingers, and he can pick up a nail with his toes.

As we go on, we notice that some Japanese methods of work seem to be the direct opposites of ours. There is a carpenter planing a board. He pulls the plane toward him, instead of pushing it from him as our carpenters do; and when he uses the drawing knife he pushes it instead of pulling it, as would seem to us to be the natural way. The American builder begins his house with the foundation. The Japanese builder makes the roof first. He puts it together in pieces upon a scaffolding of poles, and then fills in the framework beneath. The logs are often brought to the building, and the boards sawed out by hand as they are needed. In the lumber yards of Japan the sawmill is an almond-eyed, barelegged man, who stands on top of a log, or beneath it, and pulls or pushes away with the saw until he has cut the log into boards.

Sawmill.

We find that Osaka has a vast trade. It may be called the New York of Japan, for it is the commercial capital of the empire. The city itself has a population of about five hundred thousand, and with the manufacturing villages which make up its suburbs, it contains more than a million people. It has many great wholesale establishments and hundreds of large retail stores.

In its stock exchanges we learn something of Japanese trade, and we find that Japan sells to other nations every

COMMERCE AND INDUSTRY. 73

year one hundred million dollars' worth of goods. We of the United States buy of Japan several times as much goods as she buys of us, and her trade with us is increasing. The chief things that we export to Japan are kerosene oil, different kinds of machinery, and raw cotton. More than half the homes of the Japanese people are now

Making Matting.

lighted by American oil; many of the modern mills of the empire have machinery from America; and millions of the Japanese working people are kept warm by cotton from our Southern States. On the other hand, our ladies use Japanese silks by the millions of yards; many of our houses are furnished with Japanese rugs made of cotton and jute; and the most beautiful matting sold in our stores now comes from Japan.

The greater part of the tea which flows down American throats is made from leaves raised on Japanese soil, and almost all the camphor used by the world comes from Japan. The United States imports tons of this drug every year, and in our tour we now and then pass great camphor trees. There are camphor groves scattered throughout the western part of the empire, the trees of which are perhaps the most valuable known to the world. In the village of Tosa, in western Japan, there is a group of thirteen trees about one hundred years old, which, it is believed, will produce forty thousand pounds of crude camphor, and which are worth, as they stand, four thousand silver dollars.

The camphor tree is an evergreen of the laurel family. It has a trunk not unlike that of an oak, and this, in full-grown trees, usually runs up from twenty to thirty feet without limbs. Above this point branches extend out in every direction, covered with an evergreen foliage, and forming a well-proportioned and beautiful tree. Some of the camphor trees of Japan are fully fifteen feet in diameter, and some are more than three hundred years old. The trees are destroyed in the production of camphor. They are cut, roots and all, into chips, and these pieces are boiled so that the camphor sap and oil are cooked out of them. The sap and oil go up with the steam, which is conducted into a vessel kept cool by running cold water over it. This condenses the vapor into a deposit of oil and camphor. The oil is pressed out, and that which remains is the crude camphor of commerce.

From Osaka, a half hour by rail takes us to Ko'be, the chief seaport of central Japan. It lies at the entrance of the famed Inland Sea, through which we pass on our way to Ko-re'a. We travel in a Japanese steamer, float-

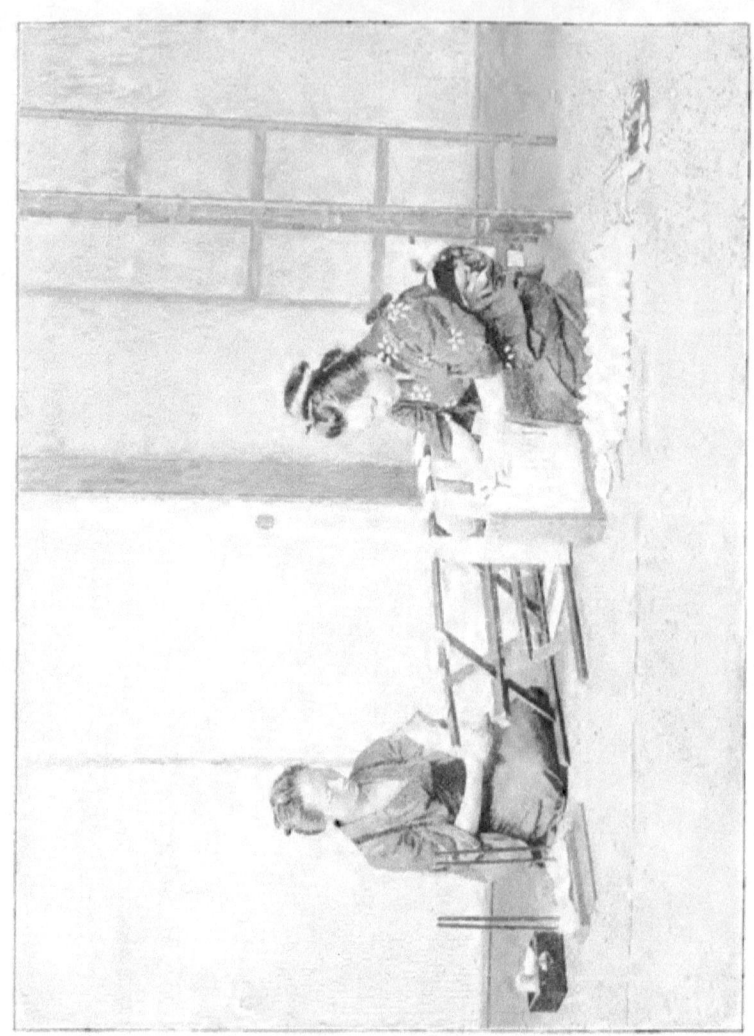

Folding Skeins of Silk, Japan.

COMMERCE AND INDUSTRY. 75

ing in and out among mountainous islands, the hills of which are terraced, and which have many black-roofed villages dotting their shores. We pass through narrow channels, moving in and out among Japanese craft. We float for hours through the most beautiful scenery, and at last find ourselves at anchor in the mountain-locked harbor of Nagasaki, the westernmost port of Kiushu. Here we take coal, hundreds of half-naked little Japanese women and men passing it in small baskets from one to another from a barge on one side of the steamer, until the coal is at last stored in the hold.

Our ship is called the Tokyo Maru (nä-roo). It is lighted by electricity, and heated by steam. We travel almost as comfortably as we did on the steamship in which we crossed the Pacific. The sailors and officers are all Japanese, and the Japanese passengers stand with us at the stern of the boat, and with us look longingly back as we steam out into the ocean, and say "*Sayonara*" (sī-yon-ä′rä), or "Farewell," to Japan.

Good by.

IX. THE HERMIT NATION.

A SHORT sail from Japan brings us to the land of big hats and long gowns, the land of the Koreans, the curious people who have gained the title of "The Hermit Nation." We knew nothing about them until a short time ago, yet they existed as a nation two thousand years before America was discovered, and their history records their doings as far back as twelve hundred years before Christ.

The Koreans have always looked upon their country as the most beautiful of the world, and have tried to keep other nations from learning about it, for fear that they might come and seize it. For this reason the Koreans have until lately driven travelers away from their shores, and when sailors were shipwrecked there, they were not permitted to leave, lest they might carry the news of Korea to their homes.

You have learned how the United States introduced our civilization into Japan. It also opened Korea to the rest of the world. In 1882 one of our naval officers, Commodore R. W. Shufeldt, was sent to this country. His vessel entered the harbor of Chemul'pho, and he there made a treaty by which the King of Korea consented to open his land to all nations. Since then travelers have been permitted to go where they please. The Koreans are now exceedingly hospitable. We shall find ourselves treated as guests, and we can learn much about this curious country.

Korea is a mountainous peninsula of about the same shape as Florida, and not much greater than Kansas in area. It is bounded on the northwest and northeast by

Manchuria and southeastern Siberia, and is separated on each side from Japan and China by boisterous seas. Its shores are rocky and peppered with islands. It contains many fertile valleys covered with rice, and streams by the hundred flow down its green hills. We shall find its soil rich, but nowhere well farmed. The climate is much the same as that of our North Central States, and we shall notice that the trees are not very different from those we have at home. In the mountains there are rich mines of gold, and valuable coal fields which have not yet been worked; and in a recent trip across the country the author saw many signs of petroleum.

Korea has numerous birds and many wild animals. We shall not dare to travel at night for fear of the tigers, and we may shoot a leopard as we ride through the mountains. The country contains about twelve million people, who live in a few large cities and numerous villages. Both the towns and their inhabitants are unlike those of any other part of the world, and we rub our eyes again and again, wondering whether we are really still on our own planet, or whether by magic during the night we have not sailed into one of the stars, or perhaps to the lands of the moon.

We sail around the foot of the peninsula and halfway up the west coast until we come to the harbor Chemulpho. This is the port for the capital, the city of Seoul (sa-ool'), which is situated twenty-six miles back from the seacoast, on the other side of a small mountain range. We see white-gowned figures walking like ghosts over the hills as we enter the harbor, and a crowd of Koreans surrounds us as we land on the shore.

What curious people they are! Many of them dress like women, but their faces are men's. They are not Chinese, and still they are yellow. They are not Japanese, though their eyes are like almonds in shape. They are taller than the Chinese we have in America, and their faces are kinder, though a little more stolid. They have cheek bones as high as those of an Indian, and their noses are almost as flat as a negro's. They are stronger and heavier than the men of Japan, and some carry great burdens of all kinds of wares.

Here comes one trotting along with a cartload of pottery tied to his back. During our journey over the mountains to the city of Seoul, men of that kind will carry our baggage, weighing hundreds of pounds, twenty-six miles for a very few cents. They will fasten our trunks to an easel-like framework of forked sticks which hangs from their shoulders, and they are so strong that they will trot over the hills as though they were loaded with feathers. Such men are Korean porters. They carry the most of the freight of the country, and they form but one class of this curious people.

with a cartload of pottery tied to his back."

At the top there is the king, who governs the country, and who has vast estates and acres of palaces. He lives in great state, and his officials must all get down on their knees when they meet him. There are nobles by hundreds, who strut about in gorgeous silk dresses, who own the most of the land, and who live by taxing the rest of the people. They are the drones of the country. They spend their days in smoking and chatting, and they fan themselves as they ride through the streets in chairs carried by their big-hatted servants.

There are government clerks by the thousand, dressed in white gowns, who earn their living as scribes for the nobles. They act as policemen and taxgatherers, and often oppress the people below them. There are farmers, merchants, mechanics, and slaves; and the men of each class have their own costume, by which we may know them. The gowns of the clerks have tight sleeves, while those of the nobles are so big that they hang down from their wrists like bags. No one can do hard work with his arms enveloped in bags, and the sleeve of a Korean noble could hold a baby.

We see servants and slaves dressed in jackets and full pantaloons of white cotton. They have stockings so padded that their feet seem to be swelled out or gouty, and almost burst the low shoes which they wear. The gowns are of all colors, from the brightest rose pink to the most delicate sky blue, and the men who wear them go about with a strut, and swing their arms to and fro, as they walk up and look at us, the strange foreigners who have come to their country.

But queerest of all, to our eyes, are the hats and headdresses. Some heads show out under great bowls of white straw as big as an umbrella, and others are decorated with little hats of black horsehair, which cover only the crown of the head, and which are tied on with ribbons under the chin. This is the high hat of Korea, which, like our tall silk hat, is considered the mark of a gentleman; and as we go on we shall find that each hat has its meaning. Here comes one of bright straw, as large round as a parasol, which seems to be walking off with the man whose shoulders show out beneath it. That man is a mourner, for, according to the Korean belief, the gods are angry with him and have caused the death of his father.

For three years after the death of a parent the Korean wears a hat of that kind. He dresses in a long gown of light gray, and holds up a screen in front of his face to show his great grief. During this time he dare not go to parties, and he should not do business, or marry. If, at the end of his mourning, the other parent should die, he must mourn three years longer; and when the king or queen passes away, all the people put on mourning for a season.

"That man is a mourner—"

But here come two men with no hats at all. They look very humble, and they slink along through the crowd, half ashamed. They part their hair in the middle, and wear it in long braids down their backs. Those are Korean bachelors, and until they are married they will have no rights which any one is bound to respect. Only married men can wear hats in Korea, and those without wives, whether they be fifteen or fifty, are boys, and are treated as such.

Married men wear their hair done up in a topknot of about the size of a baby's fist. This is tied with a cord, and it stands straight up on the crown of the head like a handle. Unmarried men and boys are obliged to wear their hair down their backs. They tie the long braids with ribbons, and look more like girls than boys. The Korean women, as we shall learn farther on, are seldom seen on the streets, and we meet only men and boys at the landing.

But let us travel over the mountains, and visit the great city of Seoul. It is the largest city of Korea, and it is the

Main Gate to the Palace, Seoul.

home of the king and his court. It is only twenty-six miles from Chemulpho, the chief seaport; but the roads leading to it are rough, and there is little traffic upon them. We ride in Korean chairs, each of the party sitting crosslegged in a cloth-lined box swung between poles and carried by four big-hatted coolies. As we go, we tremble at the prospect of not reaching Seoul before dark, for we know that we shall have to stay outside all night if we get there after sunset.

The Korean capital is surrounded by a massive stone wall as tall as a three-story house, and so broad at the top that two carriages abreast could easily be driven upon it. This wall was built by an army of two hundred thousand workmen five hundred years ago for the defense of the city, but it is in good condition to-day, and it can be entered only by the eight great gates which go through it. These gates are closed every night just at dusk by heavy doors plated with iron, which are not opened again until about three o'clock in the morning. The signal for their closing, as for their opening, is the ringing of a big bell in the center of the city, after which those who are outside cannot get in, and those who are inside cannot get out.

We know but one word of Korean, which means "go on," or "hurry." We cry out this word again and again, until we are hoarse. Our coolies go on the trot, and we reach Seoul in time to climb to the top of the walls and take a view of the city before the gates close.

Seoul lies in a basin surrounded by mountains, which in some places are as rugged and ragged as the wildest peaks of the Rockies, and which in others are as beautifully green as the Alleghanies or the Catskills. The tops of these mountains rest in the clouds, and as we look we see watch fires burning upon them, and learn that these form the telegraph system of Korea. They are the last of a series of fires which flash from hill to hill all over the country and by their number and size tell the king whether the people of his various provinces are at peace or about to break out into war. The wall around the city

a view of the city — "

climbs upon these mountains. It bridges a stream at the back. It runs up and down hill and valley, inclosing a plain about three miles square, in which lies the city of Seoul.

What a curious city it is! Imagine three hundred thousand people living in one-story houses. Picture sixty thousand houses, ninety-nine out of every hundred of them built of mud and thatched with straw. Think of a city where the men are dressed in long gowns, where the ladies are not seen on the streets, and where the chief business of all seems to be to smoke, to squat, and to eat; and you have some idea of Seoul.

It is altogether different from our cities of the same size. Cut the houses of a great American city down to the height of ten feet, and how would it look? Tear away the walls of brick, stone, and wood, and in their places build up structures of cobblestones put together with unburnt mud. Slice the big buildings into little ones, and move the mud walls out to the roadway. Next, run dirty ditches along the edges of the now narrowed streets. Cover the houses with straw roofs, and over the whole tie a network of clotheslines; and you have a general idea of the Korean capital.

As you look, you think of a vast harvest field filled with big haycocks, interspersed here and there with tiled barns, and with a great inclosure of more imposing barns under the mountains at the back. The haycocks are the huts of the poor, the tiled barns are the homes of the nobles, and the great inclosure contains the palaces of the king. The nobles live in large yards back from the street. Their houses look much like those of Japan. They have walls of paper between the rooms, and they are heated by flues which run under the floor. The huts of the poor, which make up the greater part of the city, are built each in the shape of a horseshoe, with one heel of the shoe resting on the street, and the other running back into the yard.

In the houses of both the rich and the poor the men live in the front, and the women are shut off in the rear. They have no views of the street except through little pieces of glass about as big as a nickel, which they paste over holes in the paper windows. The doors which lead into these houses are of the rudest description. They are so low that you cannot go in without stooping. At the foot of each door a hole is cut for the dog, and every Korean house has its own dog, which barks and snaps at foreigners as they go through the streets.

But, as we are looking over Seoul, the sun drops down back of the mountains. The great bell in the center of the city peals out its knell, and the keepers close the gate doors with a bang. Similar ceremonies are going on at the other gates of the city, and that bell, like the curfew of the Middle Ages, sounds the close of the day. We climb down the steps on the inside of the wall, and take our seats again in our chairs. We do not go to a hotel, but our coolies take us to the home of the American minister, who is a friend of the author, and who entertains us during our stay.

" — a hole is cut for the dog — "

X. TRAVELS AMONG THE KOREANS.

THIS morning we are to explore the strange city of Seoul. A Korean who speaks English acts as our guide, and we are escorted also by two of the native soldiers who are furnished to our legation by the king. There is no danger, but appearances are everything in Korea, and great people, among whom we are now classed, since we are the guests of the minister from the United States, never go out without soldiers and servants about them.

We have to watch where we step. The streets in most parts of the city are narrow and winding, and the sewage flows through them in open drains which take up much of the roadway. There are no waterworks in Seoul except the Korean water carrier, who almost fills the street as he goes from one part of the town to the other, carrying his two buckets, hung one from each end of a pole across his back. The clouds are left to do the work of sprinkling the streets, except here and there, where the servants take dippers and ladle the dirty water out of the sewers to settle the dust.

The smell is disgusting at times, and mixed with it just now is smoke, for all Seoul is cooking its breakfast. Each of the huts has a chimney which juts out into the street at right angles with the wall, about two feet from the ground. The people use straw for fuel, and this produces the great smoke which the chimneys are pouring out into the streets.

Our eyes smart as we walk on through the city. We try to keep out of the way of the porters, the water carriers, and the people who are going to the markets, which are situated at the foot of the chief business street, and about the gate through which we entered the city. We follow the crowd, and soon find ourselves in the busiest place in Korea.

There are thousands of men in all sorts of costumes, selling and buying. There are porters by scores who have brought loads of fresh fish from the seashore on their backs over the mountains, and there are butchers by dozens who are selling beef, venison and other kinds of game. There are booths devoted to the selling of rice. White-gowned men squat on the ground with bushels of red peppers before them. There are boys peddling Korean matches, which are shavings with their ends dipped in sulphur, and which have to be touched with a burning coal before they will light. There are hundreds of men buying grain, and carrying on all sorts of wholesale and retail business.

The sales are not large, and things are bought by handfuls rather than bushels. Some articles seem very curious. Eggs are sold by the stick, ten being laid end to end and wrapped around with long straw "Eggs are so tightly that they stand out straight and stiff. sold by the A stick of ten eggs brings about three cents. Here is a man selling pipe stems. The most of them are as long as himself, for the Korean gentleman's pipe is so long that he has to have a servant to light it, as he cannot reach out to its bowl when the stem is in his mouth.

See that man in a black hat and white gown, with a pile of clubs before him! They are not unlike baseball bats, and we wonder if our American game has not been brought out to Korea. We ask our guide, and he tells us that those are ironing clubs, and shows us how the women use them for ironing. The clothes are first washed in cold water and dried on the grass. They are then taken into the house and wrapped around a stick, which is laid on the floor. Now one or two women squat down before the stick, and pound upon the cloth with these wooden clubs until it becomes as smooth and as glossy as the best work of an American laundry.

" — and pound upon the cloth

Our guide points to his own gown of snow white, and tells us that it was ironed in this way, and as we go on through the city we hear the musical rat-tat-tat which comes from the ironing. This noise is to be heard throughout Seoul at every hour of the day, and during nearly every hour of the night. The garments are such that they must be ripped apart whenever they are washed. It takes a long time to iron them, and when they are finished they must be again sewed together, so that you see Korean girls have quite as much to do as our girls at home.

We learn that only the higher-class women receive any education, and that very few know how to read. After girls are seven years old they must stay in the women's quarters in the backs of the houses, and must no longer play with the boys. The noble women will not go out on the street except in closed chairs, and the poorer women whom we meet during our tour have green cloaks thrown over their heads, which they hold tight in front of their faces, with just a crack for the eyes. This is so that the men may not see their beauty as they go through the city.

A Korean Lady.

Leaving the markets, we walk through the crowd up the street till we come to the little temple containing the bell which sounds the opening and closing of the gates. This is in the business center of the city, and the streets surrounding it are thronged with merchants and peddlers, with dandies and loafers, from sunrise to sunset. The ordinary Korean store is a little booth or straw shed which juts out into the street, and which contains, perhaps, a bushel-basketful of goods. The merchants wear white gowns and black hats, and we see them squatting outside their stores with their hats on, smoking as they wait for their customers.

About the little temple there are large buildings or

bazaars, each of which is devoted to the selling of one kind of goods. These buildings have many little rooms, each the size of a very small closet, and every little room is a store. The merchants sit in the halls outside the closets, with their hats on, and bring out piece by piece as you order. They are by no means anxious to sell, and the more goods you want, the higher the price they will ask.

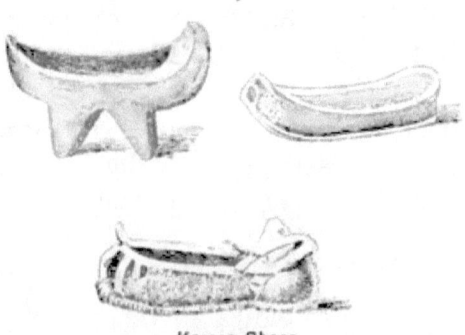

Korean Shoes.

You may get one pair of shoes, for instance, for fifty cents, but if you want a hundred, the merchant will be very sure to charge you at least a dollar a pair, on the plea that if he sold all his goods he could not keep his store open.

"Peddling candy."

A great deal of peddling is done by boys, some of whom have fires on the streets, on which they roast chestnuts to sell hot from the coals. We meet little fellows everywhere peddling candy. They have trays which hang from their shoulders at right angles with their waists, and their money boxes consist of pieces of twine, upon which they string the Korean "cash" which serve as the money of the country. These cash are about the size of an old-fashioned red cent, with a square hole cut out of the center. It takes more than two thousand cash to equal the value of one of our dollars, and we find that in taking a long journey we must have an extra bullock, or a couple of porters, to carry the money we need to use on the way.

What is the noise we hear coming from that little hut just off the main street?

That is a Korean school. The teacher squats on the floor in a gown of white or of some bright color. To-day he wears rose pink, and he has a cap of black horsehair. The glasses of his spectacles are as big as trade dollars,

"— studying their lessons out loud."

and his appearance is very imposing. His scholars squat about on straw mats studying their lessons out loud. They sway themselves back and forth as they sing out again and again the words they are trying to learn, all shouting at once. If one stops, the teacher thinks he is not studying, and calls him up for a whipping.

At our request, the teacher shows us how scholars are punished. A little fellow, well knowing that he has done nothing wrong and will not be hurt, stretches himself on his stomach flat on the floor, while the teacher takes a rod and taps him a few blows on the thighs. We laugh. The little Korean laughs, too, and when we have given him a handful of coins worth about a cent of our money, he runs back to his seat, the happiest, as well as the richest, boy in school.

The studies of Korean boys are made up chiefly of learning by heart the sayings of great Chinese scholars. They do not now have the advantages of our American children, but important changes are going on in the country, and the little Koreans will probably soon have schools like our own.

It is through public examinations in the grounds of the palace, that the officials of the country are chosen. The Koreans have great respect for good scholars. They are lovers of poetry. Young men often have poetry parties, where each guest shows his skill in writing verses upon a subject given out at the time.

We find other curious customs, some good and some bad, which have grown up during the ages the Koreans have lived by themselves. The people have much natural refinement. They are intelligent and kind, and, as we travel among them, we feel that with a good government, new laws, and equal rights for all men, such as they may have in the future, they will make as respectable a little nation as can be found anywhere.

We feel sorry to leave them, but we must go across the peninsula to the east coast, in order to get a ship for Siberia. We travel on ponies, riding for seven days up and down the mountains, passing through thousands of rice fields, and now and then skirting the wilds where we dare not go after dark for fear of the tigers. We find numerous villages of thatched huts, and notice that the farmers live in villages and not on their farms. We stop sometimes at Korean inns, where we sleep on the brick floors, half baked by the straw fires beneath us. Sometimes we stay with the magistrates, who, on our departure, as a mark of honor furnish us with trumpeters to toot us out of the town.

At last we reach the fine harbor known as Gensan. Here we board a Japanese steamer on its way from Nagasaki to Vladivostok (vlä-dĕ-vŏs-tōk'), and after a few days' sail northward we find ourselves at anchor in the Gulf of St. Peter the Great, with the largest seaport of Siberia lying before us.

Plowing in Korea.

"There is a Russian church—"

XI. SIBERIA AND THE TRANS-SIBERIAN RAILROAD.

VLADIVOSTOK is the key to eastern Siberia (see map on p. 301). It is the great seaport of Russian Asia, and is one of the most strongly fortified towns on the globe. The Gulf of St. Peter the Great, in which we come to anchor, is surrounded by mountains. At the foot of these, running up the sides of the hills, stand hundreds of wooden and brick houses. They look more like those of an American town than the structures of paper and frame in Japan, or the mud huts of Korea which we have just left. There is a Russian church, and we see many business places not unlike our stores at home.

The harbor is filled with steamers. Russian men-of-war lie beside us, and the hills are covered with barracks, in front of which Russian soldiers march up and down. Siberia is governed by Russia, and about three fourths of its five million inhabitants are of Russian birth.

The czar is trying to people the country with Russians, and among the ships which lie between us and the city we see large emigrant steamers which have come from the Black Sea, through the Straits of Bosporus, over the Mediterranean Sea, through the Suez Canal, and around southern Asia, bringing Russian farmers to Siberia. The steamers will carry them from Vladivostok one thousand miles further north, and land them at stations along the great Amur (ä-moor′) River.

Siberia is a very rich country. It is of vast extent, and it is said to have enough good soil to support a great people. It is not all a snow-clad desert, as many suppose, but it has plains and plateaus covered with grass, upon which hundreds of thousands of horses and cattle feed during the summer. It contains many coal mines, and the iron of the Ural Mountains is of very fine quality. Large deposits of gold are found in many parts of Siberia. There are valuable gold fields in the Altai (äl-tī′) Mountains, in the Urals, and in the mountain chains of eastern and southern Siberia. There are now about forty thousand miners at work, although in some places the gold-bearing soil is so frozen that fires must be built upon it before it can be dug up for washing. Nuggets of gold weighing a quarter of a pound have been found, and the grains of Siberian gold are said to be on the average larger than those of any other part of the world.

The country of Siberia is so large, and it has so few people, that we do not know just what it contains. The land is in the form of an irregular plain, sloping northward to the sea, and is made up of three long belts.

The first belt, lying along the edge of the Arctic Ocean, is frozen and bleak during most of the year. Upon this no trees grow. The land is swampy in the summer, and in the winter the Arctic Ocean freezes for a distance of hundreds of miles from the shore, and both land and sea are so coated with snow that you might ride for days without knowing where the land ended and the ice began. This is the land of the reindeer, the polar bear, and the black fox. It is the land of long days and long nights, the land where there is nothing but darkness for several weeks during midwinter, and where midsummer is one long day, in which the sun never sets.

South of this region, there is a great belt made up of almost impenetrable forests, filled with wild boars, wolves, and all kinds of fur-bearing animals. Siberia has sables whose furs are worth almost their weight in silver. It has numerous otters and squirrels, and the beautiful white ermines whose skins are used to line the cloaks of kings.

The third belt is that nearest China. This contains the farming lands of Siberia, and upon it will be located the vast population which the country will support in the future. This region has many post stations. The Russians travel through it in winter on sledges drawn by relays of horses, which gallop swiftly over the dazzling white snow. Clad in two coats of fur, the traveler is able to withstand the cold, and by rubbing his nose and ears now and then, he keeps them from freezing.

At this time the rivers are covered with ice many feet thick. Men can ride in sleighs for miles on the Amur, which is one of the great streams of Asia, and on the ice they can cross Lake Baikal, one of the largest lakes of the world. They go through mountains as picturesque as the Alps, and pass rapidly over the vast plateaus which will sometime be covered with farms.

It is through southern Siberia that the Trans-Siberian railroad is now being built. This road will be 4696 miles long in Asia alone, and when connected with the European lines it will form the longest continuous stretch of railroad in the world. It will be one of the great

"The trains are already running"

trade routes of Asia, and vast quantities of the silk and tea which are now carried by ships around that continent, through the Suez Canal to Europe, will pass over it in the near future.

The work of building is now going on along different parts of the route, and we may find hundreds of Russians at work grading the road and laying the rails. The eastern end of the railroad is at Vladivostok, and the western end is at Cheliabinsk', in the Ural Mountains. The trains are already running over the first eastern section, and we can take a ride upon this, one of the greatest trunk lines of the world.

We first explore the city of Vladivostok. It is a slice of Russia in Asia. It contains a mixed population of about twenty thousand Russians, three thousand Koreans, an equal number of Chinese, and thousands of Russian soldiers. Its streets are filled with long-bearded men wearing black caps and thick coats which reach to the tops of their high leather boots, in which are stuck their full pantaloons. We ride up the hills in droskies, or Russian carriages, drawn by black horses which gallop like mad. Our drivers speak only Russian; and, as they do not understand English, we direct them which way to go by motioning to the right or to the left.

A Drosky.

Our first call is upon the police. The government is exceedingly strict. You can do nothing in Siberia without applying to the officers, and if we would take a ride on the Trans-Siberian railroad, we must first get a permit from the chief of police. Armed with this, we go to the station, which is much like an American railroad depot, except that it is filled with soldiers, who tramp up and down, and who look fiercely at us as we purchase our tickets. We find a soldier who speaks English, and he shows us the way to our train. We ask for the sleeping cars, but are told there are none as yet, and that the only cars used are third class.

" — we go to the station — "

If you could take an American freight car, seat it with wooden benches, and above them put wide shelves running across it from one side to the other, you would have a car much like the one that we take for our journey. We find the lower seats filled, and are told by our friend that the shelves are the upper berths, and that we must sleep upon them.

The train leaves at midnight. It is lighted by candles and heated by a wood stove which stands at the end of the car nearest the engine. The Chinese, Tartars, and Russians, who occupy the lower benches, are snoring, and we climb upon the shelves and lie down. We bundle up our coats to use them as pillows, and try in vain to make ourselves comfortable. We turn over and over again, seeking the soft side of the boards, and every moment we find bones aching which we never imagined existed. The road is new, and the cars jolt up and down as they bump over the rails.

We ride in this way all night, and wake up in the morning in the midst of great plains, the soil of which is as black as your boots. We travel for miles over meadows and great fields of wheat. We find that the Siberian Russians live in villages made up of log cabins, and we are told that the lands are held in common. The

Siberian Elders.

elders or chief men of the towns divide the farms among the people year after year, and the men of each village all work together.

We stop for a time at Nikolsk, a town of perhaps ten thousand people, which looks very much like one of our new towns of the West. Here are more barracks of soldiers, and all along the line of our journey we find soldiers who evidently wonder what we Americans are doing in Asia, and who seem to suspect us as spies.

They want to know all about us, but they speak nothing but Russian, and our conversation is carried on by signs.

We look in vain for the convicts who we have supposed were to be seen in all parts of Siberia. The worst convicts are now taken to the island of Sakhalin (sä-kä-lēn′), northeast of Vladivostok, and they are not forced to work on the railroad, as they were in the past. But we see many Chinese, and at some of the stations find a few of the queer Siberian natives who make up a part of the population of this far-away land.

We learn that many of the native tribes have curious customs. For instance, the Buriats (boo′rĭ-ats), who live near Lake Baikal, are fond of horses, and when a man dies they kill a horse in order that its spirit may carry him on his long journey through the land of the hereafter. These people have slant eyes, thick lips, and snub noses. They shave most of their heads, and wear the remaining hair in queues, like the Chinese. They are fond of tobacco, and Buriat children of eight or nine years go about with pipes in their mouths.

Another tribe is that of the Tunguses (toon-goos′ez), who live in the Amur valley and in other parts further north. Some of these people are breeders of stock, but the greater part are nomadic hunters. They roam through the woods without tents, living for the time in caves or hollow trees. They travel from one part of the country to another on sledges pulled by reindeer, and they raise and breed reindeer for sale. They are very fond of animals, and those branches of the Tunguses which have fixed settlements often have menageries of bears, foxes, and wolves.

In northern Siberia there are people who are much like those we have in Alaska, and who live in tents made of skins; and the island of Sakhalin has natives similar to the hairy Ainos of Yesso in northern Japan. There are curious tribes in western Siberia, which we may visit by going northward from the Caspian Sea, after we have traveled around Asia by way of China, Siam, and India. Just now the great Empire of China lies almost south of us. Were the Trans-Siberian railroad completed, a branch line would probably be built through the Great Chinese Wall, and in less than a day we could go by rail to Peking. At present the sea is the only safe route, and we take the railroad back to Vladivostok, where we catch the Russian steamer, which, sailing southward around the Korean peninsula, will land us in China.

"— live in tents made of skins —"

A Chinese Family.

XII. CHINA — A TRIP TO PEKING.

TO-DAY we begin our travels among the Chinese. They are more than one fourth of all the world's people. They have yellow skins, black hair, slant eyes, and little fat noses with very broad nostrils. The men and boys shave their heads, with the exception of a spot on the crown, as big as the palm of your hand, from which a long braid of hair, called a queue, hangs down the back. The women have very small feet, made so by having been bound so tightly from childhood that they have been unable to grow; and the hands of both women and men have long, slender, tapering fingers. The men often dress in long gowns, and the women, in some **parts** of the country, wear pantaloons.

These people have many curious customs, and we shall find ourselves traveling through a new world. It is a great world, too. The Chinese have vast cities, in which there are hundreds of workshops, banks, schools, and all sorts of stores; and we shall find the people everywhere

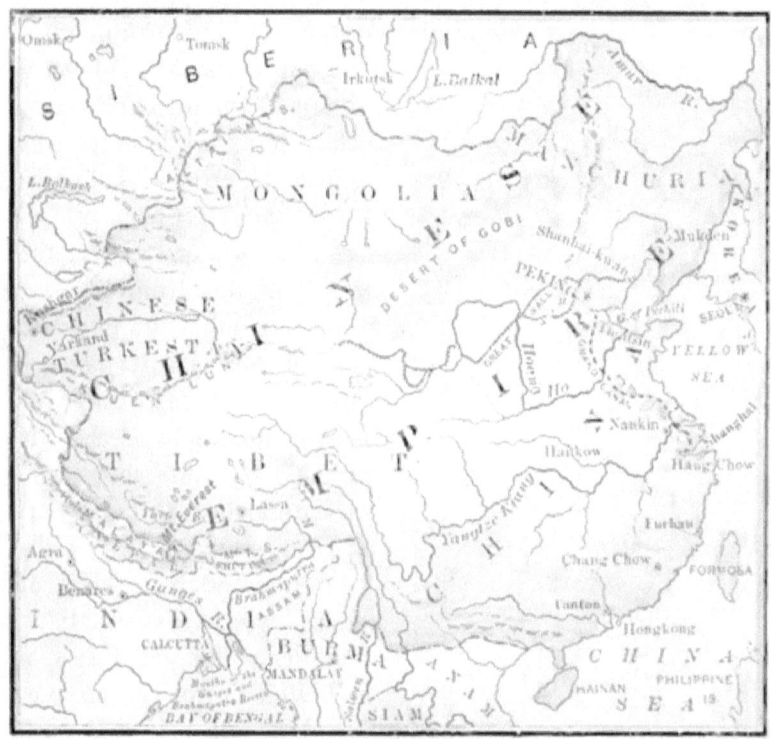

The Chinese Empire.

working. Their minds are as bright as our own, and when we trade with them we shall have to look out or they will get the best of the bargain. They are an old people. They had a civilization long before Rome was founded, and they have numbers of villages which were in existence hundreds of years before Columbus discovered America.

The Chinese have one of the greatest and richest of all the countries in the world. Their empire—which consists of China proper and the vast tributary provinces of Manchuria, Chinese or Eastern Turkestan, Mongolia, and Tibet—is one third larger than the United States. It has millions of acres which have for centuries produced two crops a year. Its mountains contain all kinds of minerals,

Winter Costume.

and there are said to be coal and iron lying near to each other in every one of the eighteen provinces which form China proper.

China proper is where the most of the Chinese live. It is not quite one half the size of our country, but it has at least five times as many inhabitants. Fully one half of it is mountainous, and the southern part is largely made up of hills. The remainder consists of plains which extend back from the edge of the sea, and which are cut up into small farms, supporting millions of people. It is a land of many climates. At the north the people dress in sheepskins during the winter, and in the southernmost parts the children often go barefooted at New Year's.

We begin our travels with a visit to the city of Peking. It is the capital of the Chinese Empire, and there is no capital in the world so hard to get at. It lies in the northern part of the country. The nearest port is Tientsin (te-ĕn'tsēn), which is situated on the little Pei (pā) River, about fifty miles from its mouth. This stream, the Pei Ho (the word *ho* means "river"), forms the only entrance to the vast country of north China. The river is narrow and winding. It curves in and out like a snake, and as we move up it we see, both in front and behind us, the white sails of queer Chinese boats apparently floating through the green fields as they pass along the course of the river.

We are entering the Great Plain of north China, which extends for seven hundred miles along the coast, and which runs from one hundred and fifty to four hundred miles back into the interior, supporting, it is said, more people than any equal area on the globe. The land is as flat as a floor, and we can see for miles on all sides. The plain is cut up into farms without fences, and spotted here and there with small clumps of trees surrounding the collections of mud huts which are the homes of the farmers.

The banks of the Pei Ho are dotted with little cities and villages. The stream is so narrow that we often float close to the houses. We observe that the walls are made, in most cases, of sun-dried bricks, and that their low, slanting roofs are composed of bundles of reeds plastered with mud. The houses are all of one story. They look more like boxes than houses, for some of them are not more than fifteen feet square. They are built close up to the streets, which are narrow dirt roads without sidewalks. In some places, parts of the buildings extend out over the banks of the river, and we are told that the freshets often wash the foundations away and drop such houses, families and all, down into the water.

We see the streets swarming with curious people. There are yellow-skinned merchants in black satin caps and gay-colored silk gowns. There are shaven-headed workmen whose queues are tied up in order that they may be out of the way, and who are dressed in blue shirts and wide, flapping pantaloons of blue cotton. There are bareheaded women in coats of green, purple, and crimson, below which show out their bright-colored trousers and little silk shoes. There are yellow-skinned boys and girls dressed like their parents, some playing about, and others watching the steamer go by. The poorer boys are more than half naked, and we tremble at their danger as we watch them wrestling together, rolling each other over and over on the banks at the very edge of the water.

The roads along the river between the towns are filled with a stream of yellow-skinned people of all classes, conditions, and ages. There are half-naked porters, who go on the trot as they carry great loads balanced on the ends of the poles which rest on their shoulders. Now and then we pass ladies on their way to a call on their neighbors. Their feet are too small for them to walk comfortably, and they ride on the backs of their men-servants, their bandaged feet in gay slippers bobbing up and down out of their silk pantaloons as they hold on by clasping their arms around the necks of the servants. There are Chinese gentlemen who are being carried along in sedan chairs swung between poles, and there are small-footed old women who walk on with canes. There are laborers and peddlers of every description, and hucksters with baskets on their way to the markets. We see hundreds of people at work in the fields, and we get our first glimpse of the industry of the Chinese, which is unsurpassed in the work of the world.

The numbers increase as we go up the river, and at Tientsin we find scores of brawny laborers ready to handle the freight at the wharves. They carry the great boxes and bales out of our ship upon poles which they rest on their shoulders, all grunting and yelling together as they raise and lower their burdens. As we look closely at them we are surprised at the size of these men of north China. They are taller than those of the southern part of the empire, from which the Chinese of America come. Some are fully six feet in height, and not a few can lift five hundred pounds each at a load.

Tientsin is the chief business city of north China. It contains more than a million people, and Peking, the great Chinese capital, is only eighty miles away. The two cities are not farther apart than New York and Philadelphia, and you would think that the Chinese would have some rapid method of getting from one to the other. A passenger train could cover the distance in two hours, but there is no railroad which goes to Peking.

Our trip will have to be made in Chinese fashion, and we find that the journey by land will require two or three days. We might go part of the way by water, taking a house boat and making a several days' sail up the Pei Ho to the town of Tung Chow, which is fifteen miles from Peking. But in this case we should have to use donkeys and carts for the rest of the trip, and if the winds were unfavorable our sailors would walk on the banks and pull the boat up the river by a rope tied to its mast. We shall therefore travel the whole way by land. We can ride on ponies or in carts, or, if we would go very cheaply, we can each hire a wheelbarrow and be pushed and pulled to Peking by men.

And do the Chinese travel on wheelbarrows?

Yes, you see people riding upon them in all the great cities. In Shanghai there are nearly two thousand passenger wheelbarrows. Vast quantities of goods are carried from one city to another in this way, and if we have a strong wind during our trip over the Great Plain, we may see some of these barrows with sails fastened to them so that the pushers may be helped on by the wind. We find many barrows with both men and donkeys harnessed in front, thus aiding the owner, who holds up the handles and shoves hard behind.

A Passenger Wheelbarrow.

The Chinese wheelbarrow is larger and heavier than ours. The wheel comes up through the center of the bed, instead of being at the front end. There is a framework over the wheel, and the passenger sits, with no support for his back, on the ledge on one side of the framework, facing the front. He rests one leg on the ledge, and supports the other foot by a stirrup of rope which is fastened to the front edge of the barrow; and he holds on by throwing his arm over the framework inclosing the wheel. Such barrows, however, are used more for freight than for passengers. They form, to a large extent, the drays of the country, and they carry much of the goods which go from Tientsin to the capital, the boxes and bales being tied to the ledges on each side of the wheel. You may see, now and then, a barrow with a hog or sheep on one side and on the other a pretty Chinese girl, who, like as not, has paper flowers in her hair and rouge on her cheeks.

the common means of Chinese road travel

I have traveled to Peking in every way except on the wheelbarrow, and by my advice we take carts. These form the common means of Chinese road travel, and they are in use all over the empire. Usually each cart is pulled by two shaggy mules, harnessed one in front of the other, and driven by a Chinaman who sits on the shafts.

What a clumsy vehicle a Chinese cart is! Its two wheels are twice as heavy as those of the carts used in the

United States for repairing the roads. The shafts are about half as thick as telegraph poles, and the bed of the cart rests upon them without springs. Above the bed is a framework covered with blue canvas which forms the roof of the cart. This is too low for a seat to be placed beneath it, and we are told to get in and sit flat on the bottom of the cart. There is no support for our backs, and when we attempt to lie down we find the bed so short that our feet hang out at the front, disturbing the driver.

The mules go on a trot, and our flesh is almost jolted to jelly by the ruts of the road. The dust is so thick that we can taste it. Our lips become dry, and when we lick them they are straightway coated with clay. We are tired out before we have ridden ten miles, and we are surprised when we learn that this is one of the best roads of China. The empire is said to have four thousand roads, but these have been so cut up by the wheels of the carts during the ages, that traveling upon them is like going through ditches. They are filled with clouds of dust when the weather is dry, and when it rains they are turned into rivers of mud.

A Hotel.

We see strange sights everywhere as we go on our way to Peking. We pass through many villages. We spend two nights in Chinese hotels, the surroundings of which make us think of a barnyard. The rooms are stablelike

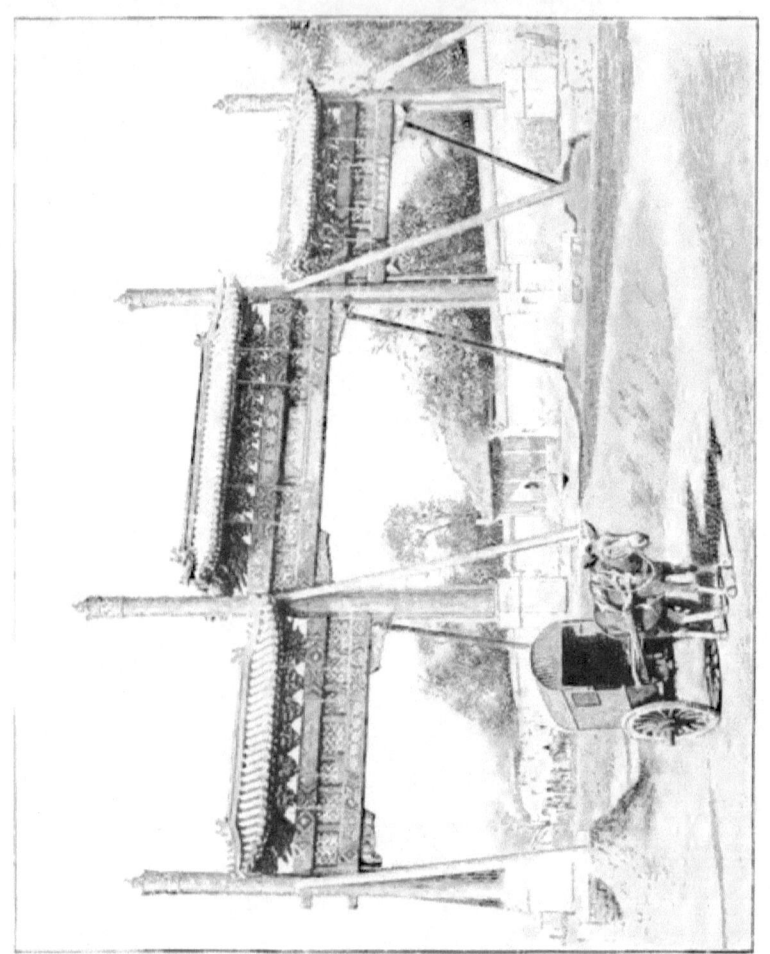

Commemorative Arch, Pekin.

sheds built about a court filled with donkeys which bray at all hours of the night, and with camels which cry like whipped babies.

Our bed is an ovenlike brick ledge about two feet high which fills one half of the room. It is heated by flues running under it. The fuel is straw, which quickly burns out; and the bed is stone cold before a new fire is lighted. We are therefore alternately roasting and freezing. There are no springs and no bedding. We turn over again and again, and at daylight get up with all our bones aching.

We start at six in the morning, and ride until dusk, and about ten o'clock the third day we find, by the increased number of wheelbarrows, donkeys, and carts, that we are nearing the great capital of China, and far off in the distance we see the walls of Peking.

XIII. THE GREAT CAPITAL OF CHINA.

PEKING is a walled city. Its million and a half of yellow people live in a vast inclosure surrounded by walls so high that you would have to climb to the top of a very tall tree to look over them. Think of surrounding New York or London by walls — not fourteen-inch walls as high as a fence, but great walls sixty feet thick at the bottom, as tall as a four-story house, and so broad at the top that you could drive four wagonloads of hay side by side upon them without crowding. Let these walls be faced inside and out with gray bricks, each as thick as a big dictionary. Let the space between be filled with earth so packed that the ages have made the whole as solid as stone. Build great towers here and there upon the top of the structure, above gates which go through it and form the entrances to the city; and you have some idea of the walls of Peking.

Such walls surround every important Chinese city, and it is estimated that there are four thousand walled cities in China. The walls were built as a means of defense. Upon some of them cannon still stand, and on others piles of stone are collected to be thrown down at the

Walls of Peking.

enemy in case of a siege. The towers were intended for watchmen, that the city might be warned of the approach of an enemy. The gates under the towers are great arched tunnels lined with stonework. They form the only entrances to the cities, being open during the day and closed at night by doors plated with iron. There are sixteen such gates leading into Peking. We can tell where they are by the towers, which we see long before we come up to the walls.

We ride for miles through the dust outside the city

and finally reach one of the gates. We are jostled by the crowds, but our cartmen push their way through the entrance, and we climb up into the tower and take a view of Peking.

What a curious city it is! It looks like an immense orchard cut up by the wide dirt roads forming its streets, through which move all sorts of animals, vehicles, and

"— and take a view of Peking."

men. The city is filled with trees, but among them we can see the thousands of one-story, stablelike structures of gray brick which make up the stores and homes of the people. Here and there a government building, shaped somewhat like a big American barn, rises above the trees; and all around, and running here and there through the whole city, are these mighty walls.

Peking is divided by the walls into three different cities. There is the great Tartar city at the north; and almost in the center of this is the imperial city, surrounded by two sets of walls, one of which runs inside of the other. The imperial city contains many palaces roofed with yellow porcelain tiles, in which the emperor lives with his wives and his thousands of servants. There is the Chinese city at the south, in which we see the temples of Agriculture and Heaven, the places to which the emperor, as the representative of his nation, goes out in an elephant cart to pray to his ancestors for a prosperous year, and where in the spring, with a gold-handled plow, he starts the first furrow, after which all the Chinese farmers begin to put in their crops.

It is in the Chinese city that the most of the business of Peking is done. The streets there are narrow, and are lined with all kinds of stores, as we shall see later on.

The Tartar city is the seat of government, and in it we shall find the real capital of China. Centuries ago the Tartars from beyond the Great Wall conquered the Chinese. They reigned a short time, and then were driven out; but a few hundred years later they again conquered, and since then the rulers of China have been of Tartar descent. The present emperor is of that race, and he has a large number of Tartars, as well as Chinese, among his officials. We shall meet many of the officials on the streets of Peking, and we shall see here types of the curious people who make up this great Chinese Empire.

Let us go down from the tower, and make our way through that crowd of pushing, howling men and beasts which moves through the gate from the Tartar city to the Chinese city from sunrise to sunset. What a wonderful collection it is! There are caravans of brown, woolly camels, on their way to Mongolia, loaded with tea, and ridden by fierce-looking Tartars. There are carts without number

PEKING, THE GREAT CAPITAL. 115

Camel and Driver.

containing the silk-dressed nobility, and there are common workmen known as coolies, half naked, on foot. There are little gray donkeys by hundreds straddled by yellow-skinned merchants, and urged on by the blows of yellow-skinned donkey boys who follow behind.

There are sober-faced scholars wearing spectacles, the glasses of which are as big as silver dollars, and there are dandies dressed in satins and silks. There are shaven-headed priests from Tibet in gowns of bright yellow, and travelers from all parts of the empire in costumes of all shades and tints. There are barefooted beggars in rags, and there are gorgeously dressed princes on ponies, all pushing and scrambling and shouting as they force their way through the gate. The busiest parts of the city have similar crowds, and we hire donkeys in order to ride through the streets.

How dirty, how vile, how shabby everything is! The streets of Peking are dirt roads full of ruts, and the carts are dragged through them with the mud up to their hubs. The streets take the place of sewers. Decent language cannot describe their condition. Pools of dirty yellow water are everywhere, and wherever we walk in Peking we have to pick our way through the filth. At night we

A Street Lamp.

must carry lanterns, for the city has neither gas nor electricity. Its only street lamps are latticework boxes, backed with white paper and raised up on a framework of poles

"The woodwork is carved"

to the height of a man's head. In the boxes are candles which are lighted at night, and which through the paper cast rays so dim that you can hardly see the ground just beneath them.

Take a look at the stores. They are all of one story, with the front room coming close to the edge of the street. There are no plate-glass windows. The light comes in through open doors or latticework walls backed with white paper. How gorgeous the fronts of the stores are! The woodwork is carved, and is painted with the brightest of colors, in many cases being covered with gold leaf. The signs are long boards of red, black, green, or gold, upon which Chinese characters are painted. The signs run up and down the sides of a shop instead of across its top, as with us. The merchants wear caps and long gowns, and they keep their hats on in the stores. They stand behind counters as we do. They are very good salesmen, but they have no fixed prices, and ask three times as much as they think you will pay.

Here and there we pass banking establishments, and at the corners of the streets we may often see money changers sitting at tables with piles of copper and brass coins before them. These coins are called cash. They form the chief money of China, and it takes about two hundred of them to equal in value one of our cents.

not more than ten dollars.

They are similar to the coins we saw in Korea, being like a big penny with a square hole in the center in order that they may be strung upon strings. Cash are heavy, and we find that thirty dollars' worth of them would be a load for a mule. Here are the author and his Chinese servant holding cash, the total value of which is not more than ten dollars. Large transactions are carried on by means of silver, which is valued by weight, a Chinese ounce being known as a tael and worth a little more than the silver in our silver dollar.

A Chinese store, as a rule, sells but one kind of goods, and stores of the same kind are usually to be found close together. There are streets lined with book stores, and in some parts of the city we find scores of hat stores and fur stores and shoe stores.

There are many things sold which would seem strange if offered for sale in America. The drug stores, for instance, have board signs advertising ground tigers' bones to strengthen faint hearts, and extracts of rat flesh to make the hair grow. There are shops which sell nothing but gold and silver paper, which the Chinese burn at the graves of the dead in order that they may not go without money into the land of spirits.

We shall find large establishments that make and sell coffins, some of which cost hundreds of dollars. The Chinese often buy their coffins a long time before death, and it is not unusual for a good son to present his father or mother with a fine coffin at New Year's. The father will keep the present in the best room of his house, and will show it with pride to his neighbors.

There are many bird stores in Peking. The Chinese are fond of pets, and we shall see old men on the streets who carry little birds about with them on sticks which they hold in their hands. The legs of the bird are fastened to the stick by a string which permits it to fly a short distance. We find pigeons sold on the edge of the markets. These birds are the messengers of Peking, and they are, perhaps, the only pigeons in the world that whistle. As they fly through the air they make a noise which on the approach of a flock sounds like a whole school of boys blowing on tin whistles. This noise comes from whistles of wood which the people tie to the tails of their birds to scare off the hawks.

There are great porcelain stores in Peking, and shops which contain the finest of silks and the most beautiful satins. There are lock peddlers by hundreds, and hardware stores. There are places where wood is sold in little bundles by weight, and where you may buy for fuel round lumps of mud mixed with coal dust, of about the size of a baseball, for a few cash apiece.

Another surprise meets us in the markets. We have thought of the Chinese as living on nothing but rice, cats, dogs, and rats, but we discover that their markets are almost as good as ours. They have the choicest of fruits, and we can buy oranges, grapes, and nuts of all sorts. They have many kinds of fish, which they bring alive to the cities, keeping them in tubs of water until they are sold. They have excellent mutton from the sheep of north China, which are of the fat-tailed variety, a single sheep's tail often weighing several pounds. They have all sorts of game, and you can buy deer and squirrels, snipe, quails, and many other kinds of birds.

One of the chief meats sold is pork. We shall see black hogs all over China. They trot through the streets of Peking, and they wallow in the puddles by the side of the road near the gates to the emperor's palaces. They seem to us the dirtiest hogs in the world, but the Chinese think that there is no meat more delicious than pork. They are especially fond of one kind of this meat which is produced on an island off the coast of south China, the pigs from which it comes being fed almost entirely on sweet potatoes and chestnuts.

As to cats, dogs, and rats, these are sometimes sold and eaten in the poorer parts of the cities. I once bought a dried rat in Canton for three cents, and I have visited restaurants where soups and stews of cat and dog meat are kept always on hand. In one place I saw a dog being cooked. The flesh looked like pork, the fur having been scalded and scraped from the skin, with the exception of a bit on the end of the tail. This bit of fur was jet black, and it was left on to show the dog's color, as the flesh of black cats and black dogs is considered the best.

XIV. THE EMPEROR, AND HOW CHINA IS GOVERNED.

FROM the walls of Peking we can see the roofs of the emperor's palaces. They are made of bright yellow tiles which blaze like gold under the sun. Yellow is the imperial color of China, and almost everything connected with his majesty is of this golden hue. When the emperor goes out into the city, the streets and roads over which the royal procession is to pass are first covered with bright yellow clay, and we may see Chinese laborers bringing such dirt into the city in wheelbarrows during our stay.

But can we not see the emperor himself?

No, such a thing is impossible. No foreigner except the ministers is allowed to call upon him. He lives in his palaces inside the walls of what is called the Pink Forbidden City, shut off from all foreigners and from even his own people. If any one dares to go through the gates of the imperial city without permission, he will be flogged with one hundred strokes of a bamboo stick upon his bare thighs; and a stranger found in the emperor's apartments would surely be strangled. Even the servants and those who have business with the emperor must have passes to go in and out, and the guards at the gates scowl at all foreigners.

When the emperor takes an airing, the Chinese officials send word to our minister that Americans will go upon the street at their peril. The soldiers at such times clear the streets of all carts. The people are supposed to remain within doors. They hang mattings up in front of their houses, and strips of blue cotton are stretched across the side streets, so that no one may look out. As the procession goes by, the Chinese get down on their knees behind the mats, and bump their heads on the ground in honor of the emperor. If, being out in the country and unable to get out of the way, they should suddenly come upon such a procession, they must at once get down on their knees and keep their heads on the ground until his majesty has passed out of sight. The emperor has soldiers with him, and he is usually accompanied by archers. These look out for sight-seers, and the man who peeps through a hole in the mats may get an arrow or a bullet shot into his eyes.

A Chinese Archer.

The Chinese call their emperor "The Son of Heaven," and they look upon him as holy. He is so great that his officials have to remain on their knees while they are in his presence. When he tried to learn English some time ago, his teachers knelt before him while they taught him his lessons.

The emperor is an absolute monarch who rules his people through many officials. He has his cabinet ministers, who preside over the government departments, and who have many officers and clerks under them. The ministers report to his majesty the most important measures for his sanction. If the emperor approves, he makes marks to this effect upon their reports with a red paint brush known as the vermilion pencil, and the measure becomes a law.

A High Official.

In a vast empire like that of China, however, only a very few of the public matters can be submitted to the emperor, and the business of the government is largely left to the officials, many of whom are very corrupt and take a large share of the public moneys for their own use. There are eighteen provinces or states in China, each of which has a governor with hundreds of officials under him. Each village has its own officers, and every family is, to a large extent, responsible for the good conduct of the neighborhood. If a boy commits a crime, his father, his elder brothers, and his teachers are sometimes punished, as well as himself; for the Chinese say that if they had taught him properly he would not have broken the laws.

All cities and villages have jails, and the punishments

connected with them are among the most cruel of the world. For small offenses the criminal must wear about his neck a frame of heavy boards called a cangue (käng). The frame is about three feet square, or about the size of the top of an ordinary kitchen table. It is made in pieces so that it can be opened and the man's neck fitted into a hole in the center. The common cangue weighs twenty-five pounds, but there are many so loaded with iron bars that they weigh as much as ninety pounds.

Now, if you will imagine your neck fastened through a hole in a kitchen table weighted with iron, you can see how you would be punished if you committed a very small crime in China. You would find that the frame extended out so far beyond your neck that you could not possibly reach your mouth, and you would have to rely upon others to feed you. You could not lie down with such a frame fastened about your neck, and if a fly or a bee happened to light on your nose you could dislodge it only by shaking your head. Upon the top of the cangue, on each side of the hole, are pasted strips of paper describing the crime committed by the wearer, and the people stop and read them as the criminal passes through the streets.

"For small offenses—"

The worst crimes that can be committed, we find, are those by children against parents. There is no other land where fathers and mothers have so much power. Parents have the right to whip their children to death if they will not obey. The punishment for striking a parent in

China is death, and if a son kills his father or mother he is condemned to execution by the slow process known by the Chinese as "ling chē." The man is tied to a cross and is slowly sliced into pieces. Only a small piece of flesh is taken off at a time, until his eyebrows, the muscles of his arms, the calves of his legs, his cheeks, and other parts of his body have been removed; and the man dies by inches, as it were, from the numerous cuts.

The Chinese, however, love their children as much as our parents love us, and it is seldom that any one becomes liable to this terrible punishment. Obedience to parents does not stop when children grow up, but it lasts until the death of the parents. Men and women are often whipped by their fathers and mothers, and a man after he is married often asks his mother's permission if he wants to go out after dark. I remember an instance which occurred during my stay in Canton some years ago. Mr. How Qua, a Chinese millionaire about forty years old, was asked to dinner by the American consul. He replied, "I think I can come, but I must first ask my mamma."

You would not suppose that any people could have such barbarous customs as the punishments here described, and still have, in some respects, a high degree of education and civilization. The Chinese, however, are full of contradictions. They are as polite to one another as any people of the world. They are fond of books, and they are great philosophers, always talking about virtue and justice.

The ruling class is made up of the scholars of the empire. Many of the highest officials have been poor boys, and the aim of nearly every schoolboy in China is to learn his lessons so well that he may become an official, for it is through good scholarship that officials are chosen.

A Chinese Girl.

GOVERNMENT AND EDUCATION.

The studies are mostly made up of Chinese history and of the sayings of Confucius and Mencius, two great Chinese scholars who lived centuries ago. The studying consists largely of memorizing the works of the great Chinese scholars, and of writing essays and poems on virtue, justice, and government. The boys also learn a little arithmetic, for which they use a framework of buttons on wires, much like the Japanese soroban. But the Chinese have no other such practical studies as we have — as, for instance, chemistry and geology.

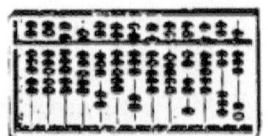

The Chinese Counting Box.

Education is confined to the boys, and few girls ever learn even to read. There are no public schools, and the teachers receive their pay from the pupils. A boy is sent to school at five or six years of age, and on the first day he carries a red visiting card with him. He also takes a present of money to his teacher. He always bows to the teacher when he enters or leaves the room. He studies out loud, and, as we go through the streets of Peking, we shall often hear a noise as though a dozen boys were fighting and howling. If we follow the noise, we shall find that it comes from a school, and that the boys are merely learning their lessons. They sit either on their heels on the floor, or on benches before tables, and they shout out at the tops of their voices the words they are trying to commit. If a boy stops shouting, the teacher thinks he has stopped studying, and gives him a caning.

Let us see how the reciting is done. The teacher calls a boy to his desk. The boy hands his book to the teacher, and then, turning his back so that there may be no chance of his getting a peep at the book, rattles off his lessons by rote.

The Chinese boy must learn to read and write the Chinese language, and he must commit to memory many thousands of verses during his school life. At about the age of seventeen he is ready to take his first public examination, and he goes to the capital of the district in which he lives. He finds thousands of other boys there. The government officials are in charge of the examination. At the firing of a cannon the boys go into great halls and sit down at tables to write essays and poems. The examination lasts several days, and it is so strict that only about one student in a hundred is able to pass. After passing this test, there is another examination at the capital of the province, and the students who are successful there have the right to go to Peking to be examined for a still higher rank.

Portion of a Chinese Book.

The Peking examination halls consist of rows of little brick cells. Each one is about big enough to form a stall for a donkey. It is open in front, but it has neither windows nor doors. The student sits on a board which is set into the wall at about the height of a chair, and he writes on another board above this which serves as a table. Each student carries his own food, candles, paper, and ink into his cell with him, having first been searched by the officials to see that he has no notes concealed in his clothes. He is watched by soldiers all the time he is in the cell, and for three days and nights he writes poems and essays upon subjects which are given out at the time. Those who pass this examination are sure of an office,

GOVERNMENT AND EDUCATION.   127

and the boy or man who stands highest is honored all over China.

At the Peking examinations there are men of all ages. Persons who fail try again and again, and grandfather and grandson often write their essays in neighboring cells. The examination is sometimes so hard that the worry and

Examination Halls at Peking.

fatigue of sitting up for three days and nights causes death; and in the walls which surround the examination halls of Peking we may see a hole where the students who die during the test are dragged out. Not long ago, a bright Chinese boy who had finished his essay grew tired and dropped off to sleep. His candle fell over and his papers were burned. He was so disappointed by the accident that he killed himself in his cell.

XV. THE GREAT WALL OF CHINA.

A RIDE of three days on donkeys takes us from Peking to the Great Wall of China. The road goes through the mountains, and is therefore too rough for carts. We have learned a lesson from the sleepless nights we passed on our way to Peking, and we carry our own bedding, which we lay on the brick floors of our rooms in the Chinese inns where we stay over night.

Our donkeys are not much larger than Newfoundland dogs. The saddles are made of a number of blankets piled up on their backs and so strapped that they stand out like flat boards. The stirrups are heavy iron rings tied to the blankets with pieces of rope. The donkeys have bridles, but these have been put on them because we are foreigners. The Chinese seldom use bridles on donkeys, and the average Chinese donkey does not understand the use of the bit. He is accustomed to being directed this way or that by a blow on the neck with a club. Each donkey is driven by a boy, who runs at the side or behind, with a stick in his hand.

In addition to our donkeys we take some mule litters, in which we can ride when we are tired. The mule litter is a sort of a kennel-like box, covered with cloth, and swung between two thick poles, each about thirty feet long. These poles stick out in front and behind, forming two pairs of shafts, in which the mules walk or trot in single file. The shafts are bound to the sides of the mules. The litter is open in front. It is furnished with blankets, and you crawl in and lie down, being jolted by the mules as they carry you over the road.

It takes us more than an hour to pass through the city

from our hotel to the gates, and outside the walls at the north we find the roads lined for a long distance with mud huts. We cross marble bridges, and soon reach the great highway which goes from China to Mongolia, and over which pass millions of dollars' worth of goods every year. Riding upon it is worse than traveling through newly plowed fields. The feet of thousands of donkeys, and of

A Mule Litter.

tens of thousands of camels, and the wheels of hundreds of rude Chinese carts have cut the road up into hollows and ruts. The bed of the road has been worn down so that in many places it is little more than a wide ditch through the fields. We are often turned out of our way by gorges and pools of half-liquid mud, and our animals are often in the mud up to their bellies. We cannot make more than thirty miles a day.

The road in some places is so narrow that we have to step aside for the caravans of camels, which in single file, with soft, velvety steps, move silently and contemptuously along. Six of these beasts are tied one to another by ropes fastened to sticks thrust through the flesh of their noses. The last camel of each six has about his neck an iron bell as big around as a stovepipe, and about a foot long. This

"— in single file —"

keeps up a dingdong as long as he moves, and announces to the Mongolian driver that his six of the caravan are all right. Each camel carries two tea boxes, one strapped on each side of his back. These bob up and down as the great beast, grumbling and whining, goes on his way. As we get further north the camels increase in number. We pass some caravans almost a mile long, and we see them far away on the horizon standing out like a long, moving fence against the blue sky of north China.

We soon come to the hills and at last arrive at the Nankow Pass, by which the caravans cross the mountains on their way to the north. This pass is the chief line of travel, and for more than ten generations its road has been trodden by millions. It is one of the roughest roads in the world. On a trip to the Great Wall I once met a foreigner who had attempted to go through with a cart. He was forced to leave this vehicle when he came to the mountains, and to hire a camel, which carried the cart through on its back.

We pick our way in and out among great stones for fifteen miles, stopped now and then by droves of black hogs and flocks of sheep with fat tails. We wind in and out along the bed of one stream after another, until at last, on the hills in the distance, we get our first sight of the Great Chinese Wall. Many times we think we are close to it, when a sharp turn shows that it is still miles away. We can see it cutting its way across the mountains, going from peak to peak, seeming almost to crawl over the hills. We finally come to the gate which leads into Mongolia. Then, going off to the side, we find an inclined plane or roadway by which we can ride on our donkeys up to the top of the wall, and explore this wonderful structure.

The Great Wall was built by the Chinese as a means of defense against the invasion of the Tartar hordes from the north. It begins at the sea and runs over the mountains clear across the northern boundary of China proper, just south of the vast tributary provinces of Manchuria and Mongolia, until it reaches the Desert of Gobi, north of Tibet. In a straight line it is more than twelve hundred miles long, and with its windings it measures, all told, a distance of about fifteen hundred miles. It is about twenty-five feet wide and thirty feet high. It is composed of a mass of stone and earth mixed together and faced with walls of gray or slate-colored brick, the interior being so packed down and filled in that throughout much of its eastern portion it is as solid as stone.

Near the city of Shanhai-kwan (shän′hī-kwän′), on the edge of the sea, a part of the wall has been thrown down;

"The Great Wall of China was built right over the mountains."

and I there found that the brick outer facing was about three feet in thickness. The bricks were fifteen inches long, seven inches wide, and a little more than three inches thick; and one which I brought with me back to America weighs just twenty-one pounds and five ounces. The top of the Great Wall is paved with such bricks, and along its northern side, throughout its whole length, there is a battlement or fortlike wall, behind which the Chinese archers lay and shot at the Tartars.

Great two- and three-story towers were built at short intervals upon the wall. They are made of bricks similar to those just described. They rise about forty feet above the top of the structure, and they have many portholes, through which you can see for miles over the country. The top of the wall is about ten feet narrower than its base, but is so wide that four horses could be easily ridden abreast along its paved highway.

The Great Wall is just about as high as a three-story house, and its width is that of the average parlor. Now, if you will imagine a solid line of three-story houses made of bluish-gray bricks, from fifteen to twenty feet wide, built across the United States from the city of New York to Omaha, you will have some idea of the size of the Great Chinese Wall. It would be far easier, however, for us to build such a line of houses than it was for the Chinese to construct their mighty wall. Our line would cross the States of New Jersey and Pennsylvania. It would cut the rolling plains of Ohio, Indiana, Illinois, and Iowa, where water is plentiful, where there is much clay, and where the railroads could be used for carrying the materials.

The Great Wall of China was built right over the mountains. It climbs the steepest of crags, and in one place it goes over a peak which is more than five thousand feet high. In some parts, there is no clay within thirty miles of it. The bricks were all made by hand, and many of the hills which the wall crosses are so steep that it is said that the Chinese had to tie the bricks to the backs of sheep and goats in order to get them to the builders. There are few cattle or horses in China, and every foot of this wall was made without the aid of machinery.

The Chinese historians say that it took an army of three hundred thousand men to protect the builders, and millions of people must have been employed upon it. They state that this vast work was begun and completed in the short space of ten years, and, as we consider it, we are more and more astonished at its construction and size. It is now in ruins throughout some parts of its length, and the portions nearest the western end, it is said, have almost crumbled to dust.

The wall has been repaired several times, but much of the structure is supposed to be almost the same to-day as when it was built. No one can stand upon it and not be impressed with the past greatness of the Chinese nation. It was built seventeen hundred years before America was discovered, when Rome was still a republic, and more than two hundred years before Christ was born. The Chinese must have had at that time a high degree of civilization in order to possess such a mighty army and be able to unite their people in such a work.

XVI. CHINESE BOATS AND THE BOAT PEOPLE.

WE leave Peking and travel for days, going south through the Great Plain to the Yangtze Kiang or Yangtze River. We are on the Grand Canal, which was built by the Chinese centuries ago as one of the trade routes of the empire. It runs from Tientsin six hundred and fifty miles southward, crossing and joining many large streams, and cutting its way through the most thickly populated plain on the globe. At short intervals along its course we find walled cities. We pass many towns; and the clumps of trees which we see scattered everywhere over the landscape, each marking the site of a little farm settlement, show us the truth of the statement that China is a country of thousands of villages.

The Grand Canal varies in width at different points along its course. In some parts it has followed the beds of rivers, and winds in and out, going for many miles without a lock. Here and there between the Hoang Ho and the Yangtze Kiang, where the land is low, the canal is built upon a raised work of earth kept together by walls of stone. Some portions of this embankment are twenty feet high, and the stream which flows upon it is at some points two hundred feet wide. In most places, however, the canal is fast going to ruin.

In sailing through the canal we cross the Hoang Ho or Yellow River, which, although more than twenty-five hundred miles long, is navigable for only small boats. We go on further south until we find ourselves in that mighty stream known as the Yangtze Kiang. Here we take a Chinese steamer, and, in company with many native passengers, sail up the river. The Yangtze is more than three thousand miles long, and large ocean steamers can pass up its course for more than seven hundred miles. Many streams flow into it, and we see the masts and sails of boats moving rapidly through these across the green fields.

From our steamer we see dikes in every direction. There are provinces in China which are cut up by canals much like Holland. There are vast territories where almost every man's house can be visited by boat, and as we go on in our travels we shall find that the greater part of China may be reached by navigable streams and canals, and that these form the highways of the empire.

Many of the great cities are built upon the banks of the rivers, and there are vast manufacturing centers every few miles. Each city is different from the others. Some, like Hankow, far in the interior on the Yangtze Kiang, have dirty paved streets, so narrow that we have to crowd against the walls to let the wheelbarrows go by. Others, such as Nankin, which is also on the Yangtze, but nearer

we see forests of masts "

the sea, have streets as wide as those we saw in Peking. In Canton, on the Pearl River, we find a great business city containing more than a million people, and in Shanghai, not far from the coast, the native city is connected with a large foreign settlement of many English, French, and German homes.

We can get some idea of the trade of the country by a look at its shipping. China is said to have more boats than all the rest of the world put together. At the walled cities which are built here and there upon the Yangtze River, we see forests of masts belonging to boats of all sizes, descriptions, and shapes. There are large Chinese junks with wide-spreading sails ribbed with bamboo, and there are small fishing boats, the sails of which are shaped like the wings of a bat, catching every breath of air as they dash along. There are barges loaded with all kinds of merchandise, and little canoes sculled by men standing up in their sterns. There are boats shaped just like a

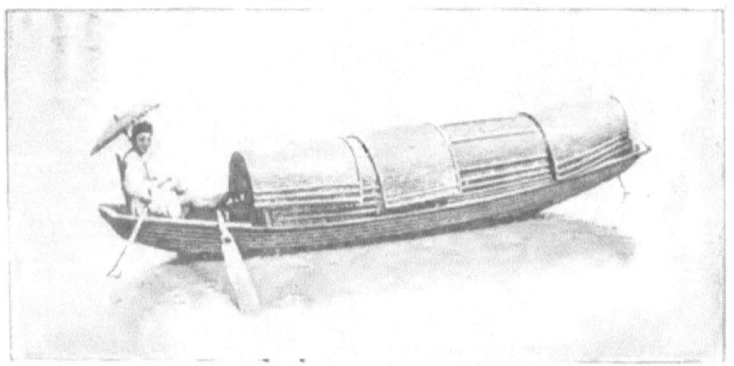

"They are used as dispatch boats"

slipper, and not much bigger than an Indian canoe. They are used as dispatch boats and can be made to go very fast. We find boats with paddle wheels at the sides turned by men who labor inside them, a half-dozen coolies doing the work of the common gas engine. There are boats owned by beggars which sail through the canals from one town to another, and lie at anchor while their owners go on shore and ask alms from the people. And there are boats filled with lepers, whom we gladly pay well to keep out of our way.

The Chinese rivers are sometimes infested by pirates

A Beggars' Boat.

who attack private boats; and during our ride up the Yangtze we see long boats and ships cut in halves and placed on end at the edge of a village or city. The owners were thieves or pirates, and the boats mark the places where the criminals have been beheaded. Their boats have been cut up in this way and put there as warnings to others. There are also vessels belonging to the river police, and customs boats whose sole business it is to collect taxes on all kinds of shipping which go up the rivers.

Each locality in China has boats of its own kind, the only thing common to all being the eyes which are painted on the sides of the prows. The Chinese seem to think that these eyes are necessary to good sailing, and that by them the boats see their way through the waters. The small boats have small eyes. The cargo boats have bigger eyes, and on some of the ships the eyes are as large and as round as a soup plate. I remember that once during a trip on the Pei Ho I happened to hang my feet over one of the eyes of the boat, and the captain rushed frantically to me and begged me to move. He said, in the peculiar English that the Chinese use in their talk with foreigners:

"Boat must have eye. No have eye, no can see; no can see, no can go."

This eye superstition, indeed, is held to such an extent that when the Chinese built their first railroad locomotive the workmen argued that it ought to have an eye painted on each side of the smokestack, in order to see its way along the track.

Most of the Chinese boats carry numerous people, and millions of Chinamen are born, live, and die upon the water. The boats are the homes of the sailors. On the Pearl River in south China, at the city of Canton, there are said to be three hundred thousand people living upon boats, and we shall find many families whose homes are boats not more than twenty feet long. On some of the larger boats the children fairly swarm, and we shall see little ones of three or four years playing about their decks. Many of the boys have little round barrels, about a foot long and six inches thick, tied to their backs. These barrels are life preservers; if a child falls everboard the barrel will keep him afloat until his mother or father can pull him into the boat.

We are surprised to see that the little girls of the boat families have, in many cases, no barrels upon their backs; and on asking the reason why, we are told that some of the poorer people consider it a piece of good fortune if their girl babies are drowned, as in this way they are saved the expense of bringing them up. I doubt whether this opinion is general, however; though nowhere in China are girls so much prized as boys. This is especially so among the boat people. I once visited a place just off the river at Shanghai, where there are perhaps five hun-

" at the city of Canton

dred Chinese babies being brought up by Christian missionaries. One of the ladies in charge told me that she could buy girl babies for from one cent to one dollar each, and she said that they sometimes bought babies, paying their mothers twenty cents apiece for them.

Among the queer boats we see on the Pearl River are those devoted to the raising of geese and ducks. The Chinese are, perhaps, the best fowl raisers of the world.

They hatch thousands of goose and duck eggs by keeping them in baskets of chaff in rooms heated with charcoal to a temperature equal to that which they would have if the fowls were sitting upon them. When the little goslings and ducklings come out of their shells, they are penned up for five days in places where they will not be disturbed by noise. They are fed at first upon rice water. After this they are given boiled rice, and at the end of two weeks they are taken out of the coop, put on these boats, and made to shift for themselves.

The boats are very clumsy and somewhat like rafts, with cooplike platforms at the side, in which the fowls stay, a single boat often holding as many as a thousand ducks. The owner of the boat rows it up and down the creeks till he comes to a low, swampy place. He then opens the fence which forms one side of the coop, a board is thrown off to the bank, and the ducks run out and pick up the worms and snails which they find in the mud. After they have fed for two or three hours the duck captain makes a peculiar call with his mouth, and the ducks are so trained that they obey his voice and return to the boat. They come very quickly, too, for the last duck always gets a blow with a stick. When the ducks are grown up, the captain carries them for sale from one market to another in his boat. There are fowl markets in all of the cities, and in Canton thousands of geese and ducks are sold every day.

In our travels through China we pass many places where the people are making porcelain and pottery. In some parts of the empire there is a smooth white clay which is used for fine china. The word *china*, indeed, comes from the beautiful work of the Chinese. According to their belief, they were the inventors of porcelain ware, and their histories state that they had china as far back as seventeen hundred years before Christ. There are now in existence beautiful china cups and vases which it is known were made centuries ago.

The fine clay of which the best china is manufactured is found in beds. It is dug out with pickaxes and carried by men on their backs to mills, where it is crushed and all the stones and sand are washed out of it. After this the clay is worked by men or by buffaloes who walk through it, mixing it with their feet; and it is then handed over to the potter. The potter molds cups, plates, saucers, vases, and other vessels from it with his hands, using the potter's wheel to aid him.

After the vessels are shaped they are put in the sun to dry and harden. Then they are glazed by dipping them into a mixture of varnish and water.

The next process is firing or baking the china. This is done in ovens which use wood as fuel. After an oven is filled with china, its doorway is closed by brickwork in order that currents of air may not affect the heat. There is only a moderate fire at first, but this is gradually increased until the pieces of china come to a white heat. The fire is kept at this point for three days, after which time the china is supposed to be thoroughly baked, and the fire is allowed to go out.

The oven, however, is not opened until twenty-four hours after this, for fear that the cold air rushing in upon the white china might make it crack. The oven cools slowly, and even a day after the fire is out it is still so hot that the persons who remove the vessels have to cover their hands with thick gloves, and their heads and shoulders with wet blankets.

As soon as the china is cooled it is given over to the

painters. Often a dozen painters will work on one piece before it is finished. One artist sketches the design, another may paint the trees and flowers, a third may do nothing but put on the butterflies, and others may be specialists at painting birds or human figures or buildings. After the china has been decorated, it must again be fired to fix the colors. This is done in circular ovens, at the bottom of which are charcoal fires.

XVII. CHINESE FARMS AND FARMING.

IN our travels through interior China we find the farmers everywhere at work irrigating their lands. The Chinese rivers bring down from the mountains vast quantities of fertilizing materials. The waters of the Yangtze Kiang and the Hoang Ho are yellow from the mud which they are carrying down to the sea, and in coming to China by water you see that the blue Pacific Ocean has been turned by these rivers to a light brown for thirty miles on each side of their mouths. The water of the Yangtze Kiang is almost as thick as pea soup. It makes the soil over which it is spread very rich. We see hundreds of men standing in pairs, here and there along the banks, scooping the thick fluid up in water-tight baskets to which ropes are attached, in order to raise it to a higher level and allow it to flow over the fields.

We see curious irrigating machines worked by cattle and by men. One kind has a rude horizontal wheel which by means of cogs turns a smaller, upright wheel, and with it a sort of a chain pump. As the wheels turn, the pump raises the water and empties it into a trough, from which it flows out over the fields. A water buffalo — an odd farm animal of which we learn more farther along in this chapter — drags the first wheel around, and thus forms the motive power. Other machines are worked by men who walk up the outside of a wheel-like framework, stepping always upward; their weight keeps the wheel

"A water buffalo drags the first wheel around"

moving, and thus raises the water. When we reflect that there are not only hundreds, but tens of thousands of men and animals engaged in such work, we see that a great deal of irrigation is carried on in China.

The Chinese are a nation of farmers. Their farms are everywhere very small, few being more than two acres in size; but they are so well tilled that one acre, it is estimated, can produce enough food for six persons. The farmers save everything for manure. Potato peelings, the hair cut from the heads of the family, the earth from the beds of canals, and the remains of old houses, as well as all other kinds of fertilizing material, are kept for the fields. We see small boys and girls raking up straw and pulling up stubble for use as manure or fuel.

Almost every kind of farm labor is done by hand. There are but few cattle, though in central and south

"- stepping always upward "

China the ugly beasts known as water buffalo are to be seen everywhere. These animals are somewhat like cows. They have flat horns which extend almost horizontally backward from just over the eyes. Their bodies are covered with a thin growth of black hair which stands out more like the bristles of a pig than the short hair of a cow. They are used for heavy work, such as irrigating, grinding meal, tramping out grain in threshing, and plowing.

"— grinding meal —"

The plowing, however, is also done with other animals, and in some places we may see men and boys hitched to the plow. On the farms of north China donkeys are sometimes used for this purpose. In a field near Peking I once saw a man and a donkey pulling away side by side, the sweat rolling down the man's face as he tried to do as much work as the donkey.

Sometimes men alone pull the plows. I remember how I photographed a Chinese father who was plowing with his two sons and a daughter, whom he had harnessed up like horses. He was pushing hard down upon the handles of the plow, and the children were straining with all their might to pull it through the furrow. When the man saw that his picture was being taken, he became very angry; for many of the Chinese believe that photography is a magic art, and that the photographer can, by willing, compel the person whose picture he has taken to come to him, and can cause him all kinds of trouble without even going near him. This plowman clearly believed that I was dealing in magic,

"— harnessed up like horses."

and he tried to seize my camera to break it. I jerked it from him and rushed for my donkey. He followed, but my Chinese servant came to my aid and held him until I was able to mount and make my escape.

The crops raised by the Chinese are of every kind and description. Much rice and tobacco are grown in central and south China, and we find wheat, barley, and other hardy grains in the north. The best tea comes from south of the Yangtze Kiang. In the city of Hankow, which is situated on the Yangtze about seven hundred miles from the seacoast, we find one of the great centers of the tea trade.

The fastest of ocean steamers are sent by the great tea importers of Europe to Hankow. The first of the crop is considered the best, and the steamers after loading run a race down the Yangtze, and through the Pacific, the Straits of Malacca, the Indian Ocean, the Suez Canal, and the Mediterranean, each trying to reach the great ports of Europe ahead of all others. The ship that wins the race gets the highest price for its cargo, as the new tea is greatly desired.

At Hankow we find vast factories in which Chinese girls are picking over tea. Their feet, which are about as big as your fist, are half covered with the leaves of the second-grade tea which they have thrown into the baskets below them. They are rapidly handling the leaves, sort-

"picking over tea."

ing over the bits of tiny green on the tables before them. The tea is fired and prepared for the market in much the same manner as we saw in Japan. It is then packed in lead-lined boxes, and we see half-naked coolies pressing it down into these chests with their bare feet.

Another great tea center is the city of Fuchau (Foo-chow). Round about it there are tea districts so large that forty thousand men and women are employed as pack animals to carry the tea to the city. Their wages are less than ten cents a day, and it costs, it is said, about two cents a pound to pick the tea.

At Hankow much brick tea is made. The leaves are ground up and steamed until they are mushy and soft. They are then put into molds about the size of a brick,

"It is then packed —"

and are pressed into shape. When they come out, they are as hard as so much pressed clay. The finer varieties of tea are molded into small bricks of just the same color, and about the same size, as the little cakes of sweet chocolate which are sold in our grocery stores. The brick tea is packed up in boxes of such shapes and sizes that they can be carried on camels into Mongolia, or on the backs of men over the mountains to Tibet. Brick tea is used in these countries both as drink and food, being cooked up with fats, as we shall learn in Tibet, into a kind of tea soup. The Mongols often use such tea as money, each brick being worth about fifteen cents.

Almost everywhere we go in south China we shall see men and women reeling and weaving silk. At Nankin

" - weaving silk."

we visit the looms where the satin dresses are woven for the emperor. The machinery is very rude. Men and women twist the thread with their hands, in the open air, and the looms from which beautiful silks and velvets are turned out are operated altogether by hand.

But where do the Chinese get the silk thread?

It comes from the cocoons of the silkworms, which feed

on the leaves of the mulberry tree. The worm spins the cocoon or shell of silk about him, and after a time, if not killed in order that its cocoon may be used for silk, it comes out a moth. There are large districts in China in which silkworms are raised, and the people think them so important that even the ladies of the emperor's court have silkworm nurseries. The empress herself, as a good example to the women of China, on a certain day collects some of the mulberry leaves, cutting them from the trees with her golden scissors, and takes them in to feed her silkworms.

But let us visit some of the silk-raising districts. We find that the care of the worms is by no means an easy task. The worms come from eggs which are laid by the female silk moths upon sheets of coarse paper; a single moth often lays as many as five hundred.

The eggs are about the size of a mustard seed, and are of a pale ash color. They are kept in a clean, cool place until the time comes for hatching, when they are put into a well-warmed room, the paper containing the eggs being laid on mats spread over shelves of bamboo wood. The temperature of the room is tested, not by a thermometer, but by a man who now and then strips off his clothes and comes in naked. By the feeling of the air upon his skin he can tell whether the room is cold or damp, and if so he heats it with stoves.

The eggs hatch within a very few days, each egg producing a little black worm as fine as a hair. Mulberry leaves cut up into very small pieces are now fed to the worms. For the first few days they get such food every half hour, day and night. As they grow older they are fed once an hour, and when they have reached their full growth they eat only three or four meals a day.

During its growth the worm takes a sleep every four or five days, and about the twenty-second day it has its last or great sleep. At this time it lifts up the fore part of its body and rests in that position. During each sleep it casts its skin, continuing the sleep until a new and larger skin is fully matured.

When the silkworm has reached the age of thirty-two days it is full-grown. It is now the color of amber, and is about two inches long and about as large round as a man's little finger. It is at last ready for the work for which it was created. It takes no more food, and begins to spin the silk from its mouth, fastening the fine thread to a frame upon which it has been placed. It moves its head from one side to the other as it spins, continuing the operation until its whole body has been enveloped in a cocoon.

The spinning requires from two to five days, and when it has finished its little silk house the worm again falls asleep. The boards upon which it lies with its sister cocoons are now carried to a slow fire of charcoal or wood, and the sleeping worms are destroyed by the heat. After this the cocoons are put into boiling water, and women and girls unwind the silk. The fine threads are reeled and twisted together until they become large enough for weaving the beautiful silks and satins which are used by the Chinese, and some of which are sent to America.

In our travels through China we also pass many thickets of bamboo. We see plantations in which the bamboo is cultivated, and we learn that it is one of the most valuable plants known to man. In some Chinese cities there are whole streets where there is scarcely anything but bamboo sold, and during our tour through the southern Asiatic countries we shall see it in use everywhere.

The bamboo is a treelike plant, which in China, Japan, and India often grows to the height of from forty to eighty feet. It has a hollow stem with joints at regular intervals upon it. You have seen cane fishing rods. The best of these are of bamboo cane. Now, if you will imagine fishing rods of all sizes and lengths, from some as thick as your little finger to others that are as large around as your leg, and as tall as a six-story house, you can get some idea of the bamboo plants of south Asia. These plants have long, feathery leaves. Their stems are green, and they do not, as a rule, turn yellow until they are cut or have become dead.

The bamboo is used for many things. Its roots, and the shoots which come up in the spring, are cooked and served somewhat like

" — we also pass many thickets of bamboo."

asparagus, and the seeds are ground up and used for food. The roofs and walls of the houses in many parts of China are made of bamboo, and there is scarcely an article of Chinese furniture of which this wood is not a part. It is used for making chairs and beds. Its splints are woven up into mats and baskets. The most of the umbrellas in Japan and China have bamboo handles and ribs, the framework being covered with oiled paper; and our paper lanterns which come from Japan are kept in shape by the little ribs of bamboo splints which run around them.

The Chinese make hats of bamboo, splitting up the wood, weaving it together, and covering it with paper. The blind beggar's stick is a bamboo cane. The washer woman's clothesline is a long bamboo pole, which, raised upon supports, holds the newly washed garments high from the ground. Many of the pens and brushes used in China are of bamboo, and some of the paper upon which the Chinese write is made of bamboo wood which has been soaked and reduced to a pulp.

XVIII. CURIOUS CHINESE CUSTOMS.

IN this, our last day among the Chinese, let us consider some of the things in which they differ from us. We call them heathen. They look upon us as little better than savages. They think we are very impolite, and pity us because we do not dress, act, and live as they do.

Long Nails.

When two Americans meet they clasp hands. When two Chinese friends come together they shake their own fists at each other, and if they are going in the same direction they walk off in single file like geese. We cut our finger nails short. The Chinese let theirs grow long, and long nails are with them the sign of a lady or gentleman. All those who do not work with their hands are proud of their nails, and the scholars, officials, doctors, and other professional men often have nails from one to six inches long. Ladies sometimes have silver shields which they put over their nails to prevent them from breaking. I met a Chinese merchant in Canton who could rest the palm of his hand upon his chin and scratch the back of his neck with his nails.

The Chinese do not kiss. They seldom embrace, and in bowing to one another they bend down almost to the ground. We take our hats off when we enter a house. The Chinese gentleman keeps his hat on. We ask first after the wives and daughters of our friends. The Chinese would consider such questions an insult, and the girls of the family remain out of the room when gentlemen call on their fathers or brothers.

A Chinaman in Full Dress.

The Chinese girls are not courted. Marriages are made by parents through professional matchmakers, and a husband seldom sees his wife until he is wedded. The wife is the slave of her mother-in-law, who has the right to whip her if she does not obey.

In China the men wear the finest embroidery, and the high officials have their hats decorated with feathers and wear strings of beads around their necks. The men often wear bracelets, and gentlemen are fond of long stockings, while their wives go about in short socks. The Chinese women often wear pantaloons, above which there is a sack coming halfway down to the knees. The men in full dress wear gowns which reach from their necks to their feet.

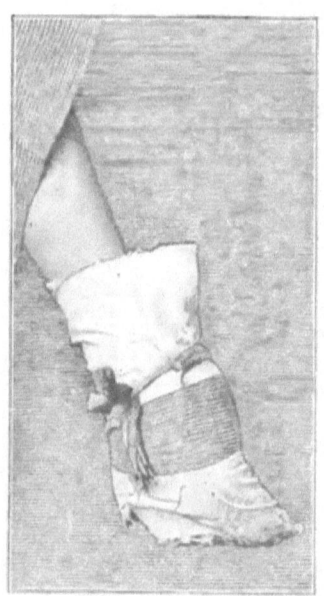
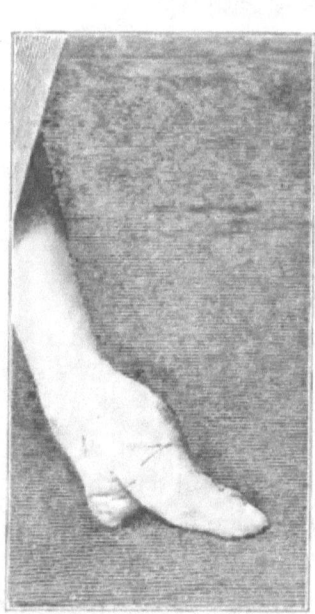

"The Chinese women are proud of small feet — "

Some of our women have the bad habit of squeezing their waists by lacing, and some Americans consider a small waist a mark of beauty. The Chinese women are proud of small feet, and they bind the heel down into the foot by tying the four small toes under it, so that their feet are much like the ends of clubs. The binding often

Chinese Women.

begins when the girls are three years of age. The bandages are kept on from that time until death, except when they are removed for washing the feet. The compression causes terrible pain, and the bandage is sometimes so tight that the foot breaks in two at the instep, the bones coming through the flesh.

We wear black when we go into mourning. The Chinese at such times wear white; and they send out mourning cards which are printed on white paper, though ordinarily the color of their visiting cards is the brightest red. After the time of mourning has half passed away they send out other cards, upon which is printed "Grief is not so bitter as before." They put on a garb of light blue for half mourning, and when the days of their mourning are ended they give a feast to their friends.

The Chinese army officials wear buttons on their caps, instead of epaulets on their shoulders, to indicate their rank. The Chinese begin their books at the back instead of the front; and in dating their letters they put the year first, then the month, and then the day.

They have many queer kinds of food. They boil their bread instead of baking it, and in north China we meet many cook peddlers who are selling boiled biscuits. The Chinese are fond of an expensive soup made of birds' nests. They eat eggs, but never serve them soft-boiled. They pickle their eggs in lime, and the older such eggs are, the better they like them. They never drink cold water, and their wine is served boiling hot.

The Chinese have theaters, but the performances are carried on during the daytime; and instead of lemonade and peanuts, they have themselves served with watermelon and pumpkin seeds, at which they nibble while the acting goes on.

They seldom wash the whole body, and it is said that many Chinamen receive only two baths while on earth, one at birth and the other when prepared for the coffin. They do not wash their hands before dinner, but a servant brings a hot, wet cloth to the guests at the table, and they rub off their hands and faces with this, passing it from one to another.

"— are usually of cloth."

The Chinese eat from tables as we do, but they use chopsticks and not forks to convey the food to their mouths. The food is served in small porcelain bowls, the meats being cut into little cubes, and the tea is served in cups with the saucers on top.

A Chinese gentleman's shoes are usually of cloth. Ours are of leather, and we black them all over; but he whitens only the sides of the soles.

"— tied to her back."

The Chinese baby has no cradle. The little one is strapped to the back of its mother, or that of a servant, and if the mother is a working woman she goes about her business with the baby tied to her back. When the baby begins to walk it is given a pair of knit shoes with a cat's face on the toes, this being supposed to render it as sure-footed as a cat. The Chinese boys fly kites, but the best kites in China are owned by grown-up men, who enjoy them as much as the boys do.

The Chinese are great gamblers. Cockfighting and quailfighting are common, and in some of the cities we see men kneeling down on the streets about little bowls in which fighting crickets are placed. The little insects are urged on to fight by being tickled with straws, and they fight until they are dead. A good fighting cricket is valuable, high bets being made upon the results of such contests.

One of the most striking features of China noticed during our tour is the terrible poverty of the lower classes of the people. The beggars exist everywhere in large numbers. Children are sometimes stolen and made blind in order that they may beg more successfully. The beggars of each city have unions or clubs, to which they all belong. They divide the city into sections, each member having his own street or block.

" thrust through his cheek."

These beggars will undergo any pain in order to excite pity. I saw at Shanghai a half-naked man, whose clothes consisted of a strip of coffee sacking wrapped about his hips. He sat on the stones with the two raw stumps of his legs stretched out before him; and his feet, which he had cut off to excite pity, were lying by his side. There is a Peking priest who goes about begging with an iron skewer thrust through his cheek. He twists this now and then so as to keep the hole ragged and sore, and he pounds upon a gong as he pushes his bloody face into yours and asks for alms.

The Chinese can live more cheaply, perhaps, than any other people of the world, and we are surprised at the saving which we see everywhere. Nothing goes to waste. The straw and the weeds, and even the leaves of the trees, are gathered for fuel. Clothing, rather than fire, is used to keep out the cold; and fuel costs so much that the poor man never builds a fire if he can help it. A large part of his diet is rice, which is cooked in quantities and rewarmed for breakfast by pouring hot water over it. The hot water used at such times and for tea is often bought from hot-water peddlers. You can get a bucket of water for one tenth of a cent, and in Shanghai there is one hot-water store for every twenty families.

At the restaurants the tea grounds are all saved, and nothing about the cookshops goes to waste. Even the water in which potatoes and other vegetables are boiled is saved and sold for feeding hogs, and the bones are cut from meat before it is sold, in order that they may be used for the making of chopsticks.

There are public cookshops and soup houses kept by charity in some Chinese cities during the winter, but as soon as spring comes these are shut up, and the poor, as we say of the horses, are turned out to grass; for they have to live on the weeds and the greens. The necessities of the Chinese are, in fact, so few that a poor man can buy enough food to keep him alive for two cents a day, and upon four dollars a month a man can support a family and put something away for his funeral.

There is no land in the world where labor is so well organized as in China. The workmen and the government have been anxious to keep new inventions out of the country. The Chinese officials are afraid to introduce railroads rapidly for fear of the anger of the wheelbarrow pushers, cart drivers, and boatmen. The opposition of these men is so great that in 1896 China had only one railroad, about two hundred miles long.

We find, however, that the Chinese are skillful in handling machinery. They have lately established large gun works for constructing all kinds of cannon, and are making Winchester rifles as good as our own. They are building their own railroad cars, and I saw a locomotive made in their gun works at Shanghai which was as good as those used in our country. They will in the future probably build more railroads. They may become one of the greatest manufacturing nations of the world, and, with their cheap labor, may at some time make all kinds of goods for the world's markets.

Chinese Boys.

XIX. SIAM AND THE SIAMESE.

AT Hongkong we take a steamship that will carry us to Bangkok, the capital of Siam. Hongkong is a little, mountainous island lying off the southern coast of China at the mouth of the Pearl River. It belongs to Great Britain, having been given up by the Chinese to the British in 1841, just after a great war which occurred at that time between the two nations. Hongkong is so near

A Chinese Passenger Chair in Hongkong.

China that you could row in a small boat in ten minutes from one point on its coast to the mainland. You could walk from one end of the island of Hongkong to the other in half a day, for it is only about eleven miles long. Its width ranges from two to three miles, and it is almost entirely made up of rocks.

You would not think such an island worth having, but it is, indeed, one of the most valuable pieces of land in the world. Its bare, bleak hills, which are from two to four thousand feet high, surround a beautiful harbor which is visited every year by more than sixty thousand ships and

LAND AND PEOPLE. 163

junks, making Hongkong one of the great ports of the world. We find at the wharves ships from India, Australia, Siam, and Java, and from all parts of Europe. Many steamers which cross the Pacific from America also end their voyages here.

The city of Hongkong is known as Victoria. It lies on the banks of this wonderful harbor, its houses covering the sides of hills so steep that, in going from one part of the city to another, we are carried up in chairs swung between poles which rest on the shoulders of half-naked Chinamen.

We find thousands of Chinese doing business in Victoria. There are about two hundred thousand of them in the city, though it is governed by officers sent out from Great Britain. We see red-coated British soldiers everywhere. The policemen are tall, black-faced, black-bearded East Indians who wear turbans of the brightest red, and who dress in long coats and pantaloons. These men are Sikhs from the British army in India.

In sailing from Hongkong to Bangkok, we skirt the eastern coast of the great peninsula known as Indo-China or Farther India (see map on p. 202). Indo-China has an area about one fourth that of the United States. It has much good soil. Its mountains contain mines of gold, silver, iron, and tin, and in its western part, in Burma, are found some of the most beautiful rubies of the world. Indo-China, however, is to a large extent a tropical jungle, in which wild elephants and tigers roam, and through

Sikh Soldier.

which crawl many kinds of venomous snakes. The country is inhabited by curious peoples, and we find that it is naturally divided into four great sections.

The eastern provinces are controlled almost altogether by the French, and are taken up by the Tonquinese, Anamese, and Cambodians. These people have all the vices of the Chinese, without their ability or industry. They have very little civilization, and as they import and export but little they are not of much importance among the peoples of Asia.

The western part of Farther India is made up of the country of Burma, which is now governed by Great Britain; the wedge of land lying between this and the possessions of France is the independent kingdom of Siam; and on the great prong on the southwestern end of the peninsula, and in the islands about it, live the Malays, who are a most curious people, with many odd customs.

We shall first visit Siam. It contains about five million inhabitants, and its area is a little greater than that of Spain. It has many rivers, and much of it is cut up by canals. It has rainy seasons, during which the streams overflow and almost the whole country becomes one vast lake. At such times the people move from village to village and from city to city in boats. The houses upon the land are built upon high posts to be out of the way of the water at the time of the floods, and to be somewhat protected from tigers and snakes. A large part of the people, however, live upon the water. The rivers and canals contain hundreds of thousands of floating houses. Bangkok, the capital, is a city of seven hundred thousand people, and it has been estimated that six hundred thousand of these live upon the water.

Bangkok lies upon the river Menam, about forty miles from the Gulf of Siam, and its floating houses extend for a distance of perhaps more than ten miles up and down the banks of the stream. Upon the land are the palaces of the king surrounded by walls somewhat like those we saw in China, the gorgeous temples of the Buddhist religion, of which we shall learn in the next chapter, and a number of stores and dwellings.

"— upon high posts —"

As we sail up the Menam in our steamer from Hongkong, we see many floating houses. The river is wide, and its banks are lined with a jungle or luxuriant growth of tropical plants and trees, in which birds of gay plumage sing, and out of which monkeys look at us and chatter as we go by. Here and there a canal goes off into the jungle, the houses floating upon it making it look like a street.

What queer dwellings these floating houses are! Let

us take a look at them as we move among them in Bangkok. They are built upon rafts from fifteen to twenty feet square. The rafts are fastened to piles, and they move up and down with the rise and fall of the tide, which is quite great even at this distance from the Gulf of Siam. Each house has a steep ridged roof, and in some cases there are two ridges, the end of the roof looking like an inverted W. Many of these houses have little verandas in front of them. All

"They are built upon rafts –"

are of only one story, and very few of them have more than three rooms.

We can see into the houses through the open doors. There is hardly any furniture. The people squat on the floor on their heels. We look in vain for sofas or beds. The Siamese sleep on the floor, and as for pillows, these are merely wooden blocks or bundles of stuffed cotton about as large as a brick and almost as hard. The cooking is done on little fires of charcoal which burn in boxes filled with ashes. There are no stoves, and the houses have no chimneys. The windows are merely open holes, and there is not a pane of window glass, I venture, in this great floating city.

Some houses, we are told, pay rent for their places on the river, but if the owners become dissatisfied they do not need to call in carts or drays in order to move. They merely untie their houses from the posts to which they are fastened, and by means of boats tow them off to other locations.

Some of the floating houses contain little stores, and the people go shopping in boats. Every house has a boat, and many children have canoes of their own. We see little naked boys rowing boats not more than two feet in width and so long that the least loss of balance would turn them out into the water.

The river is filled with boats of all kinds. The most of them are managed by women; and as we go on we find that the women of Bangkok do more than their share of the work, and that the men loaf, smoke, and gossip, while their wives earn the money required for the family. There are hundreds of peddlers' boats rowed by girls who move along from one house to another with vegetables or trinkets for sale. There are great freight boats rowed and sculled by half-naked women who stand up as they push the oars to and fro. There are boats worked by wrinkled old women of sixty, and boats filled with crews of women and men carrying merchandise through the city. The whole river is alive with boats, which dart this way and that, moving in and out among the houses.

What an odd city it is, and how queer are the people! The Siamese are of the Mongolian race. They have yellow skins. Their eyes are slanting, much like those of the people of Japan and China. They have thick lips, and their noses are almost as flat as those of a negro. Their hair is jet black, but we see many old Siamese whose heads have become as white as snow. Both men and women wear their hair short all over their heads, and it stands straight up like the bristles of a shoe brush.

What queer clothes they wear! Some of them are half naked. Many Siamese boys and girls under ten years of age wear nothing at all but a piece of twine about the waist. To this string small charms are fastened to keep off the witches and spirits. Even the children of very rich people wear no clothing at times, for at a great celebration I once saw a little Siamese prince strutting about with nothing on him but a belt of woven silver an inch wide bound round his waist, and anklets of gold on his legs and rings on his fingers.

Siamese Man.

The men of the poorer classes wear little more than a strip of cotton cloth a yard wide and two yards in length. This they wind tightly around the body just above the hips, twisting one end through between the legs and tucking it in at the waist. Some have another strip of cloth which they throw over their shoulders, and the richer men wear jackets of cotton or silk in addition to the garment which thus takes the place of our pantaloons.

The women clothe the lower part of the body in much the same way as the men. They sometimes wrap a wide band of cloth about them under the armpits, and fasten it in a knot just over the chest; but the poorer classes of women are often bare to the waist. The babies we see on the verandas of the houses wear little more than the yellow powder which their mothers have dusted over their bare skins to keep off the flies and mosquitoes.

There is a family at dinner.

They squat on their heels on the floor about a little table not more than a foot high. Their meal consists of pickles and rice, and the rice is brought to the dinner in the kettle in which it was cooked. All eat with their fingers. Each sticks his own hand into the kettle, and takes out all he can hold, rolling the mass into a hard ball with his fingers, and then cramming it into his mouth. The men and boys are always served first, and the women take what is left.

Siamese Women.

All classes seem to have plenty to eat. The wants of the people are few, and fruits, vegetables, rice, and fish are the chief foods of the country. The use of meat is contrary to the principles of the Buddhist religion. The Siamese believe that the souls of men after death go into the bodies of animals, and hence they do not eat flesh.

We are disgusted with even the prettiest of the Siamese girls when they open their mouths, for their tongues and teeth are as black as your boots, and not a few have mouths filled with what seems to be blood. We see that all men when not eating are chewing, and that some now and then spit out great quantities of blood-red saliva. We find that this comes from the chewing of the betel nut, a custom which is common throughout Farther India, and which is universal among all classes of people in Siam. The Siamese have a proverb which states that any dog can have white teeth, but only those who can afford to chew the betel nut can have beautiful black ones.

The betel nut grows on a kind of palm tree. It is about the size of an American black walnut. It has a green skin, is of a soft, spongy nature, and has a bitter taste. Its use has much the same effect as tobacco upon those who chew it, taking away hunger and stimulating the nerves. A Siamese cuts off a piece of this nut, and adds to it a pinch of red lime and a bit of tobacco. He puts this mixture into his mouth, and chews and chews. The betel juice and the lime color the teeth black.

Betel chewing is a vile, filthy habit, and it has changed the Siamese from a handsome people into a most ugly one. Babies are given betel nuts to chew before they are able to talk, and old women have betel nuts pounded up in order that they may roll them about over their tongues between their toothless gums. Nearly every person in Siam carries a box containing betel nuts with him. Smoking is as common as betel chewing, and all Siamese — men, women, and children — smoke cigars and cigarettes.

XX. THE KING OF SIAM AND HIS ROYAL WHITE ELEPHANTS.

THE King of Siam is the absolute ruler of the five million people who make up the Siamese nation. The country and the people are supposed to belong to him. His subjects are required by law to work for him during a part of each year. He can throw any man into chains or put him to death; he can deprive him of his property, or have his daughter sent to the palace as one of the royal wives.

The king has immense palaces built on the banks of the Menam River in Bangkok. These buildings cover many acres, and the walls about them are several miles long. Inside the walls there is a little city laid out in streets. Many of the buildings are of foreign style. Some of them are never entered by any man except the king. These are the quarters devoted to the king's wives, of whom his majesty, it is said, has several hundred. At the head of them is a queen, who by law is the king's half-sister. All the ladies of the palace have short hair, like the other women of their nation. Many of them have foreign dresses, but they usually wear the ordinary Siamese costume, adding to it a jacket of silk and a scarf around the shoulders.

The ruler of Siam until recently made his subjects crawl about on their knees and bump their heads on the floor when they appeared before him. It was King Chu-la-lang'korn, who ascended the throne in 1868, that first allowed his subjects to stand in his presence. He introduced many improvements, including a post office, a mint, and an agricultural department. There is now a street-car line on the land part of Bangkok, and a little railroad has been built. There is, however, great room for improvement in the condition of Siam. The people are sunk in superstition, laziness, and vice. Gambling is common. Very few Siamese are educated, and of the rich lands of the valley of the Menam only about one twentieth is cultivated.

we come to an immense building

But let us visit one of the king's palaces. We pass soldiers at the gate as we go through the wall, and after a short walk we come to an immense building of brick and stone covered with stucco, a kind of plaster. It is painted white, and under the bright rays of the Siamese sun it appears to be made of marble. It has several stories, and wide marble stairways lead up to a great front door. The stairways are guarded on each side, at the bottom, by elephants of iron plated with gold.

We walk between these elephants, pass up the steps, and soon find ourselves in one of the most splendid rooms of the world. It is the state reception room of the king. Its walls are frescoed with gold. Its ceiling is of pieces of glass of all colors, which, with the light shining through them, look almost like jewels. At the back of the room is

THE KING AND HIS ELEPHANTS. 173

the king's throne, with the state umbrellas decorated with silver and gold standing beside it. These umbrellas are held over his majesty when he receives his subjects.

All around, placed against the wall, and half filling the room, are trees and bushes of the precious metals. The leaves of these trees are of solid gold and solid silver, and the trunks are of wood or metal plated with gold and silver. The workmanship is as beautiful as that of the most skillful jewelers of Europe.

This is, perhaps, the most valuable collection of trees in the world. It is composed of the offerings made by the king's officials and by the rulers of his tributary provinces. They make him presents of gold and silver trees every year, and in this way he gets a large part of his wealth.

The King of Siam is, indeed, a very rich man. His income is said to be about ten millions of dollars a year. He is rich, however, at the expense of his people, the most of whom are very poor, and many of whom are in debt. Just outside his palace walls, I once saw a number of Siamese men with chains about their legs, working upon the roads.

" with chains about their legs."

I was told that they were slaves who had been made such because they could not pay their debts.

Siam is called the "Land of the White Elephant." This beast is considered royal, and his majesty, the king, has elephant stables in his palace grounds. We see pictures of elephants upon all the flags, and the figure of this animal is stamped upon the coins. When the king and the princes go out to ride in state in the streets of Bangkok, they sit in cars placed upon the backs of elephants; and

"they sit in cars placed upon the backs of elephants — "

at such times the people honor the elephants quite as much as the king.

The reason for this we find in the religion of Siam, which is a form of Buddhism. Among the Siamese, as we have seen, the souls of men at their deaths are supposed to go into the bodies of animals, and each elephant

THE KING AND HIS ELEPHANTS.

by this theory has the soul of some man in it. The souls of very good men go into the bodies of white animals, and those of good kings or saints are supposed to be born again in white elephants. These animals are therefore worshiped as containing the spirits of departed heroes. The Siamese have always treated them with great honor, though they seem to show less reverence now than they did in the past. In former years, white elephants had their special attendants. Their skins were covered with cloths of velvet, and their ivory tusks were bound with gold bands. Shows and concerts were given in their honor. Gold chains hung from their necks, and they had a number of royal servants to wait on them. We have heard these stories, and we leave the gorgeous room of the golden bushes and go out to find the white elephants.

What do we see?

Nothing but four wild-eyed, scraggy-looking beasts, with long tusks and with skins not much whiter than those of the elephant in the traveling circus. The only parts really white are their long, flapping ears. The rest of their skins is white only in spots, and we learn that a white elephant is, in fact, a sick elephant. The whiteness comes from a skin disease, and not from any king or hero, as the Siamese suppose.

As we see how the king's elephants are kept, we doubt whether his majesty, himself, believes that they are of royal blood. The stables are dirty. The animals are chained by the feet to wooden posts, and the men who take care of them are half naked and quite as dirty as the elephants. As we look, one of the keepers holds out his hand for a present of money. We give him a few coins, and he thereupon makes the royal white elephant get down on his knees to us, so that we feel quite grand for the time.

Now, let us visit some of the Buddhist temples and learn something about this religion of which we see so much in our tour through the Far East. The religion of Buddhism was founded by a prince named Siddhartha (sid-där'thä), who was born in India in the sixth century before Christ. He saw the poverty, the evil, the wickedness there was in the world, and he went forth from his palace as a beggar and wandered over the earth seeking to learn how to relieve it. After a time he thought he had discovered the true religion, and he called himself Buddha, which means "the enlightened." He then went about preaching what he believed, and thus founded the Buddhist religion, which is supposed to have more than three hundred million followers.

Buddha said that when men died their souls went into animals and insects, and that they possibly might be born again as men, but that man's future state will be good or bad as he is good or bad in this world. He taught gentleness, kindness, and brotherly love, but the sum of his religion was that life is a bad thing at best, and that heaven will be a place where man will neither worry nor rejoice, and where he will be as near nothing as possible.

This religion, however, has changed until it has become little more than a worship of idols. In Bangkok we shall find some of its most gorgeous temples and we shall everywhere meet its priests.

There are more than ten thousand Buddhist priests in Bangkok. They are of all ages from sixteen to eighty, and by a custom of the country every man at some time of his life expects to be a priest. The priests shave their heads. They wear strips of yellow cloth wound around their half-naked bodies. Yellow was the color chosen by Buddha as a sign of humility, because when he was alive the thieves and criminals of India wore yellow clothes. The Siamese priests we find far from humble. They strut about with cigars or cigarettes in their mouths, chewing the betel as they go from door to door, or float from house to house, begging for rice and presents.

Every morning they make a tour of the city, each priest having his own rice beat. The people bring the rice, already cooked and steaming, in pots, to the fronts of their houses, and when a priest comes along they fall on their knees and raise their hands as though praying, and ask him to accept the gift. The priests are considered holy, and mothers often thus bow down to their sons who have gone into the priesthood.

The Buddhist temples of Bangkok are gorgeous beyond description. They are vast buildings covered with white plaster and painted in many colors, with spires taller than the tallest of the palm trees. Some of the temple spires are plated with gold, and one temple, in which the king worships, has a golden spire that cost one hundred thousand dollars. The doors of this building are of ebony inlaid with mother-of-pearl, and one of its rooms has a carpet of woven silver.

The temple contains an idol twelve inches high and eight inches wide which is made of pure gold and jewels. When the metal was yet liquid in the melting pot, so the Siamese say, sapphires, rubies, and diamonds were stirred into it, and out of the mixture were made the hair and collar of the idol. It is before this image that the king comes every morning to pray, and here the ladies of his palace bend their knees at certain times of the year. The idol is on a pedestal which stands high above the floor of the temple. It has a little silk scarf about its neck, and we are told that the king crawls up on a ladder three times every year and changes the scarf, giving the idol a new dress for each season.

We find other idols of all sizes, and in one temple at Bangkok there is one of the largest idols of the world. It is known as the Sleeping Buddha. It is one hundred and fifty feet long, and the soles of its feet measure eighteen

"— spires taller than the tallest of the palm trees."

feet from toe to heel. A room eighteen feet wide makes a good-sized parlor, and you could not put the two soles of this idol's feet on a floor less than eighteen feet square. The arm near the elbow is as big round as a large oak tree, and the ears, if placed upon end on the floor, would reach about four feet higher than the average ceiling. This immense figure is made of clay plated with gold, and it must have cost a great sum of money.

XXI. SINGAPORE AND THE MALAYS.

LEAVING Bangkok, we sail for five days to the southward over the Gulf of Siam to the Straits of Malacca, and land at Singapore, within eighty miles of the equator. The voyage is far different from our trip across the Pacific. It is through summer seas, and our surroundings are those of the tropics. All nature is changed. At night the stars seem to be more brilliant than we have ever seen them before, and Venus and Mars cast rays like those of the moon upon the water. The moon itself appears to be closer to the earth, and larger and brighter than it was in America.

We see the stars which make up the Southern Cross, and which are not visible from our part of the world. The Milky Way seems more milky than ever. The sea is bluer, and before the moon rises the flashes of phosphorus upon the water mark out the ship's track as a wide road of fire which loses itself now and then in the darkness, but which springs alive again upon every wavelet that is sent back by the steamer.

The sun, so hot at midday that we dare not step out upon the deck without some head covering, goes down in the west in a gorgeous splendor unknown to the northern Pacific. Its dying rays color the water with bright tints of gold, which fade one into another, and finally, when the sun has sunk below the horizon, change first to a delicate purple, and then to a rich, dark blue, only to light up again under the bright tropical splendor of the moon and stars. When there are clouds in the sky the sunsets are grander. As we near the coast and float into the Straits, the sun's last rays are filtered through palm trees, and the funeral song of the dying day is sung by a thousand birds, whose voices are new to the ears of the people of temperate zones.

We have now reached the land of the Malays.

We float along the Malay Peninsula, which, though it is near the main line of ocean travel, is but little known to the world. It is in the heart of the tropics, its rich soil being covered with a dense jungle of luxuriant vegetation, and its shores bordered with cocoanut palms which may be seen by thousands with the glass as we sail by. This part of Indo-China has also forests of the choicest hard woods.

We are now in the home of the snake and the tiger. The Malay Peninsula contains jungles filled with wild beasts. Hundreds of tigers, it is said, swim across the narrow strait between the peninsula and the island of Singapore every year. During a visit which I made to the city of Johore, on the Malay Peninsula, I was shown the tracks of a tiger in the dust of a sawmill. The tiger had called the night before, but had gone away without eating up any of the Malay babies living in the huts surrounding the mill, and without playing with the quiet buzz saw. Nevertheless, the mill was in the heart of a large city, where you would not think a tiger would dare to go.

The danger from tigers and snakes is so great, we find, that the Governor of Singapore gives a reward of fifty dollars for every tiger killed, and that venomous snakes are paid for according to their size, the rewards ranging from fifty cents to five dollars. At Singapore I once saw a man bring in from the jungle thirty-nine venomous snakes, for each of which he demanded a reward. He carried them in a bag, and when he showed them to the policeman, he put his hand into the bag and pulled the snakes out one by one and killed them by cracking their heads against the ground. Why he was not bitten I do not know. He did not seem to be afraid of the snakes, although his hands were bare.

The island of Singapore belongs to Great Britain. Like the island of Hongkong, it is very valuable, though it is quite small. It is only about fourteen miles long, but it has a great seaport, the city of Singapore. This city is the halfway station on the trip around the world from America. All the great ships which trade with China and Japan stop here on their way through the Straits of Malacca. There are weekly steamers to Batavia, the capital of Java, and Borneo is not far off to the eastward. It is a thirteen days' voyage from Singapore to Calcutta, in Hindustan, and almost every day ships come to this point from Ceylon. The result is that the population of the city of Singapore is made up of natives of all these countries, and you find in it a mixture of yellows and blacks, of Hindus (hĭn'dooz) wearing turbans, and of Chinese with pigtails, of coffee-colored Malays, and of pale-white Caucasians from Europe.

When the British bought the land in 1824 it was only a flat jungle, and the town of Singapore was scarcely more than a village. It has now grown into a rich city. The island of Singapore, together with the territory on the adjoining mainland, forms the colony of the Straits Settlements, which numbers over half a million inhabitants; and the trade of Singapore amounts to more than one hundred million dollars a year, about four million dollars' worth of goods being sent annually from it to the United States.

It is from Singapore that we get many of our spices. Upon the islands about the Straits of Malacca we can visit nutmeg groves, clove plantations, and large vineyards from which come our white and black pepper.

A pepper vineyard looks much like a hopyard. The vines grow very fast. They are trained upon tree stumps, or upon sticks stuck upright in the ground.

The vines begin to bear in the third year, and they produce crops thereafter for a number of years. The best of them yield two crops a year, and a single plant

A Pepper Vineyard.

often produces two pounds of pepper in that time. Black and white pepper grow on the same vines, but the black kind is made from the pepper berries which are picked when green and turn black, while the white pepper comes from the ripe berries, which when picked are of a fiery red color. The berries are soaked in water, when the red or green outer skin falls off and leaves the pepper of commerce.

A large number of the people of Singapore are Chinese,

and on nearly all the islands of the Pacific, if we visited them, we should learn that Chinese merchants do a great part of the business. There are, in fact, almost as many Chinese in Singapore as Malays.

The Malays have inhabited the Malay Peninsula and the islands about the Straits of Malacca for more than two thousand years. They are by no means so civilized as the Chinese, although they look somewhat like them. The Malays we see at Singapore are very lazy, and we

A Malay Family.

learn that they live from hand to mouth, working only enough to keep themselves from starving. They have but little clothing, the children of the poorer classes going naked, and the men wearing a baglike skirt which reaches from the waist to below the knees. When a Malay dresses he places his skirt on the floor and steps into it, lifting it up to his waist and fastening it there in a knot by a peculiar twist. The dress of the women covers nearly the whole of their bodies, and the richer girls have light silk shawls upon their heads. The skins of these people are brown. Their foreheads are low and their forms are slender.

Malay Women.

The Malays are Mohammedans. They believe in the religion of Mohammed, of which we shall learn more further on in our travels. They keep their women secluded, and it is only those of the poorer classes whom we see on the streets.

Malay villages are made up of one-story huts thatched with palm leaves. The houses are seldom more than fifteen feet square. They contain but little furniture, the kitchen outfit consisting of little more than an iron pan and a cocoanut ladle. The family squat down on their heels or sprawl at full length when taking their ease at home, and the beds are mats spread on the earth floor.

The Malay men are very proud and haughty. They stand very straight, and their walk is quite graceful.

The climate about the Straits of Malacca is such that one needs little clothing. We are now near the equator, where the sun rises and sets at the same hour each day the year through, where the flowers always bloom, and the trees are always green. Birds by the thousands sing all the year round, and the temperature from one year's end to the other is that of a moist July.

In riding over the islands we pass through tropical jungles and through cocoanut and coffee plantations. The green cocoanuts hang by bushels in great bunches from the tops of tall palm trees, each of which is from fifty to one hundred feet high, having a trunk which is sometimes two feet in thickness.

The coffee estates are made up of fields of green bushes which, if not trimmed, grow to a height of eighteen feet. The coffee berries grow close to the branches. When ripe, they are dark red and about the size of a cherry. Each berry contains two seeds surrounded by pulp, and these seeds are the grains of coffee.

XXII. BURMA AND THE BURMESE.

THINK of a nation of eight million people, whose women wear plugs in the lobes of their ears as big round as your finger, and whose men have their bodies covered with tattooing from the waist to the knees. Let these people have olive-brown complexions, eyes almost straight, fat noses, and lips a little thicker than ours. Let both sexes have long black hair, which they bind up in a knot on the tops of their heads. Let the men wear turbans of bright red or yellow, and let the rest of their clothing consist of a white linen or cotton jacket reaching to the waist, and a gay-colored silk or cotton skirt which falls to the feet, and which is bound tightly about the legs and loins and tied in front at the waist. Let the women dress in much

Burmese Girl.

the same way, except that their heads have no covering. Let both sexes go barefooted; and you have some idea of the people of Burma, among whom we find ourselves after sailing along the east coast of the Bay of Bengal and up the mighty Irawadi River to the city of Rangun (see map on p. 202).

Burma is about twice as large as the island of Great Britain, and it is naturally one of the richest countries of the world. Its broad valleys are cut up by canals, and they produce quantities of delicious rice. It has mines of rubies and sapphires, and its mountains contain gold, silver, and copper. It has many thatched villages, and several large cities. Its former capital, Mandalay, has nearly two hundred thousand people, and there are about one hundred and forty thousand in the city of Rangun. The Irawadi River, which runs through Burma, is one of the great rivers of the world, being navigable for small boats for a distance of nine hundred miles.

Burma now belongs to Great Britain, and is governed as a part of British India.

The Burmese have their own civilization. They have their own language and literature, and we find the people far better educated than the Malays or Siamese. Nearly every Burmese man knows how to read and write. Every Burmese boy is expected to go to school. The schools are held in the Buddhist monasteries, and the priests are the teachers. The boys squat on the floor while in school, and they study out loud, shouting out the lessons they are trying to learn. The teachers have long whips in their hands and walk up and down the room watching the pupils, and the boy who stops shouting is liable to get a cut of the whip. The studies are largely made up of the precepts of the Buddhist religion, and many of the boys become priests after they leave school.

Burmese girls are seldom taught

A Page from a Burmese Book.

to read; for, according to the Buddhist belief, woman is naturally sinful, and it hardly pays to educate her. The only girl schools of Burma are those of the missionaries and some which have been established by the British rulers.

A Burmese boy's chief ambition is to have a rich coat of tattooing. He looks upon this as a sign of manhood, and gladly submits to the pain which he must undergo to secure it. The tattooing is done by a professional tattooer, who uses a steel pricker which has at its end four split points as sharp as needles. These points are dipped into ink and then thrust into the skin, carrying the ink under the surface. The tattooer takes up the skin in his hand and pinches it while he thus marks it with the inked needles which are to discolor it forever. He makes pictures all over the boy's thighs in this way, so that when the tattooing is completed the boy or man looks as though he were dressed in kid tights covered with red and blue figures of serpents, tigers, ogres, and demons. Such tattooing is not done all at once, but figure by figure, as the boy or man can stand the pain. It takes some years before one can get a full coat.

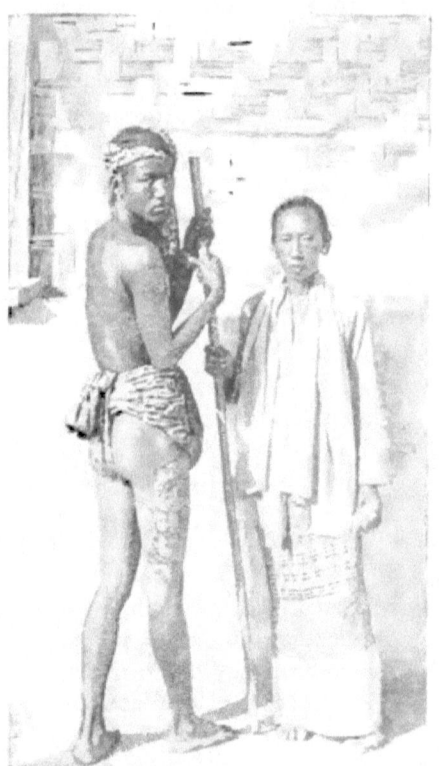

Mother and Son, the Latter partly tattooed.

The Burmese are very superstitious, and they believe that some tattooed figures will ward off certain diseases and accidents. One figure, for instance, they think is a protection from snake bite, and another, it is thought, will even save a man from drowning. Several years ago a man so tattooed was persuaded by his friends to test the fact as to whether this was true by permitting his hands and feet to be tied and himself to be thrown into the river. It is needless to say that the current carried him away, and that neither the man nor his tattoo was ever seen again.

Another kind of tattooing is of value to schoolboys. It prevents, so they think, the boy's feeling the whip when he is punished at school; and one of the best authorities on Burma states that the Burmese boys are very anxious to have figures of this kind tattooed upon them.

The Burmese women look upon the wearing of ear plugs much as the men do upon the possession of well-tattooed skins. A girl is not thought to be a woman until her ears are bored, and we therefore find that Burmese girls are as anxious to wear ear plugs as our girls are to have their first long dresses.

The making of the holes in the ears begins when the girl has reached the age of twelve or thirteen. All the sisters, cousins, and aunts are invited to be present, and a big feast is prepared for the occasion. The girl lies down on a mat, and a professional ear borer thrusts a gold needle through the lobe of each of her ears, twisting it around so that it forms a gold ring, which is left in the ear. In the case of the poor, silver needles are used. The girl screams with pain at the time of the boring, but her cries are drowned by the music of a band which plays outside the house.

It takes the ear some time to heal, and then begins the process of making the holes larger. When the ear is perfectly well, the needle is taken out, and a fine gold plate, tightly rolled up, is passed through the hole. This is gradually opened from week to week until the hole has been stretched by it to the size of your little finger, or larger.

The poor, who cannot afford gold, put stems of grass into their ears, inserting one stem after another until they have a bunch as big around as your thumb in each ear.

After a long time, when the holes have become of the proper size, the girl puts into them ear plugs or hollow pipes of gold and silver about the size of an open-ended thimble. Sometimes the plugs are set with jewels, and sometimes plugs of glass or of amber are used. In some cases the holes in the lobes of the ears become so large that a man could put his thumb through them without trouble; and I have seen Burmese women carrying cigars and cigarettes in them.

"— several plugs in one ear."

You would not suppose that the flesh can stretch as it does. Some of the poorer women's ears are so enlarged by this process that the string of flesh that hangs down in place of the lobe is almost as large round as the ear itself. In Upper Burma holes are made and plugs are worn in the other parts of the ear as well as in the lobes, and many women wear several plugs in one ear.

But let us take a look at the Burmese houses. They are in most cases little more than sheds set upon piles. They have walls of plaited or woven bamboo, and their roofs are thatched with palm leaves pinned to rafters of bamboo cane as big round as fishing poles. Very few of the houses are of more than one story. Each is built upon a platform so high above the ground that in many cases you could walk under it without stooping. Cattle and horses are often kept in the space under the house, and you climb stairs to get to the first floor.

The Burmese use but little furniture. They sleep upon mats just as the Siamese do. They keep their heads off

Burmese Houses.

the floor by resting them upon little pillow frames of cane, each pillow being about the size and shape of a small loaf of bread. The cooking is usually done out of doors. The fire is built upon the ground, and the cooking utensils consist of little more than two or three earthen pots.

The chief article of food is rice, a huge platter of which is cooked for every meal. In addition, there is a bowl of curry, a gravylike mixture made of fish and seasoned with pepper until it is exceedingly hot. The rice dish is placed on the floor, and the family squat around it, each member having two bowls, a small one for curry and a large one for rice. There are no knives and no forks. Every one helps himself, putting his fingers into his rice bowl and taking up as much as he can squeeze into his hand, and then crowding it into his mouth.

At the close of the meal every one is required to wash his own dishes. No drinking is done during the meal, but at the end of it each of the family goes to the water jar and rinses out his mouth. Every one, from the gray-haired grandfather to the boy of ten, takes a smoke after the meal, the women and girls joining in with the rest. Several of them sometimes use the same cigar, passing it from one to another and smoking by turns.

The Burmese people are very hospitable, and, with all their queer customs, they are kind and polite. The women are bright and intelligent, and the young ladies of Burma are among the most beautiful women we meet in our travels.

"among the most beautiful"

The Burmese women have more rights than any of the other women of Asia. The Japanese wife is addressed as a slave by her husband, and she seldom appears in the room when he has guests. The Korean lady, as we learned in Seoul, cannot go on the street except in a closed chair, and the small-footed Chinese wife is the servant of her mother-in-law. The Siamese girl is expected to do more work than her brothers, and she is, according to law, the property of the king. The Malay wife lives secluded in the house of her husband, and millions of the women of India and Turkey are not to be seen upon the streets. But the Burmese women mix with the men everywhere. Burmese wives have equal rights in property and social standing with their husbands, and they generally have charge of the family purse.

A large part of the business of Burma is carried on by women. The stores of each city are collected together in what are known as bazaars, each consisting of a large number of little stores or shops under one roof. The stores are small rooms opening upon the streets or passages which run through the bazaar. Each room is walled with goods. The merchants sit on the floor as they show their wares to the purchasers, who stand in the passages and bargain as to the price they shall pay. In most of the stores of Rangun the merchants are women. They sell silks, cottons, cigars, jewelry, and many other articles. Some of the women are old, but most are young girls, who, though they cannot read or write, are able to count very quickly, and who understand how to bargain.

Girls often go into the bazaars and remain there selling goods until they get husbands. In Burma love making is carried on in somewhat the same way as with us, and the Burmese husband has, as a rule, but one wife, though more are permitted. Parents often arrange marriages without asking the consent of their son or daughter who is to be married, but elopements are common, and engagements are sometimes made by the young people themselves.

The marriage ceremony consists of the eating together of rice out of the same bowl in the presence of friends, and of promising before them to live together henceforth as man and wife. The Burmese believe that women should marry, as will be seen from one of their proverbs, which reads as follows:

"Monks are beautiful when they are lean, four-footed animals are beautiful when they are fat, men when they are learned, and women when they are married."

XXIII. BURMESE FARMING AND THE WORKING ELEPHANTS.

ONE of the great sights of Burma is the elephants at work.

Elephants at work? I hear some one ask. What do you mean? Do these great, clumsy beasts actually do anything except carry men on their backs?

Yes, indeed. They are big, but they are not clumsy. They are among the most intelligent animals of the world. Let us visit the lumber yards at Rangun. There we shall find these beasts carrying great logs. They move piles of lumber, and they obey the orders of their masters almost as though they were men and could understand what was said.

Have you ever heard of the teak tree? Its wood is as heavy as iron. It is one of the finest trees of Asia. It is large and straight and very valuable. Great quantities of teak wood are shipped from Rangun to all parts of the world for use in shipbuilding and in the making of furniture. In the lumber yards at Rangun we find many heavy teak logs which have been brought there to be sawed into boards and beams for the market. Among these logs we see great elephants moving about and doing all sorts of work.

There is one carrying a log on his tusks. The elephant has thrown his trunk over the top of the log, and he balances his long, heavy burden in the air as he moves slowly onward, picking his way in and out through the piles of lumber. His master is a dark-skinned, half-naked man, dressed in a white waistcloth and jacket, and with a red handkerchief tied about his black head. He sits on the animal's neck just back

Elephant carrying a Beam.

of the great, flapping ears, with his bare legs hanging down on each side. He speaks to the elephant now and then, and when the animal does not obey he thrusts into the elephant's skin the point of a short brass hook fastened to the end of the stick which he has in his hand.

We follow the elephant to see what he will do with the log. He carries it to the sawmill on the opposite side of the yard. Here there is a truck upon wheels so placed that the logs upon it can be moved against the circular saw by which they are to be divided into boards. The elephant carries his log to this truck. He places it lengthwise upon the truck, and with his tusks and his trunk moves it into just the proper place for the saw.

There is another elephant piling logs. He has laid the logs regularly one on top of another as evenly as though he had calculated their order by measure. See how he raises that log on his tusks in order to carry it to the pile! He goes to the center of the log and gets down on his knees before it. Next he thrusts his tusks under it, and then, throwing his trunk over the top, rises slowly upward with his heavy burden nicely balanced, and thus carries it to the pile. At first he can roll the log on the others without trouble, but as the pile becomes higher he has to lift the log to the top. First he stands it upon end, propping it against the pile; then, placing his tusks under the lower end of the log, he slides it up off the ground and sends it flying into place.

" - piling logs."

In other parts of the yard we see elephants gathering up the scraps of lumber and the loose boards. They lay these in piles upon ropes which have been placed on the ground. The workmen tie the ropes around the little piles, whereupon the elephants push their tusks under the ropes and thus carry the bundles of lumber off to their proper place in the yard.

There goes a bell! It is noon, and that is the signal for the men in the yard to stop work for dinner. We find that the elephants stop, too. They do not wait for orders from their drivers, but, as the first sound of the bell falls on their ears, they drop their loads and bolt for the feeding shed. Their drivers tell us that they cannot make the animals work after the bell has been rung, and we learn from them some other curious facts concerning these beasts.

We find, that, though elephants are very strong, they are subject to many diseases, and that they must be watchfully cared for. The working elephant is fed regularly. He has his bath twice a day. He becomes very restless if anything gets under the cloth upon his back, and he will tremble like a woman at the sight of a mouse, for fear that the little animal may run up his trunk.

"He has his bath"

As we leave the lumber yards we throw some silver to the rider of one of the elephants. The man catches it. He speaks to his elephant, and the great beast throws his trunk high up into the air and gives us a salute, as though he knew that we had been kind to his master.

Elephants are used in clearing Burmese land of forests. They drag out the logs, and with heavy plows they are able to break up the matted soil of the jungle, in order that it may be turned into farms. The elephant plow is a two-wheeled instrument with a heavy share fastened to it. One man holds the handles of the plow and presses the share into the earth. Another sits on the neck of the elephant, and a third, walking by his side, aids in directing the great animal along the furrow.

Traveling in Upper Burma is done upon elephants. They are the only beasts by which we can make our way through the jungles. They can pull the branches aside with their tusks, and push their way through the thickest of the tropical vegetation. They can swim rivers and climb hills; and it is said, that, when they come to very steep places, they sometimes sit down on their hind legs and slide downhill in preference to risking a fall by walking.

The Burmese are Buddhists.

Near the city of Rangun we shall visit a great monument which was erected to Buddha, and which is one of the most splendid buildings of the world. It is a great gilded tower, rising in mighty rings from an immense stone platform, and growing smaller as it goes upward, until at last it ends in a golden spire which seems almost to pierce the sky. It is higher than any structure in America except the Monument at Washington, and the whole of it blazes in the sunlight as though it were of solid gold. Upon its top there is a golden umbrella which is studded with precious jewels. The tower is made of brick and mortar, and only its outside is plated with gold. It has been regilded again and again, and there is an enormous amount of the precious metal in it.

It was built ages ago, and the spot which it covers has been a shrine, or praying place, for more than five hundred years. During the last century one of the kings of Burma vowed that he would give his own weight in gold to it. The vow cost him forty-five thousand dollars' worth of gold leaf, for it took just that much, it is said, to equal his weight. The Burmese tell us that this Golden Pagoda is built above a casket containing two hairs from the head of Buddha himself. It is this fact that makes the place holy.

Scene in Mandalay, Burma.

FARMING AND ELEPHANTS.

About the Golden Pagoda we find dozens of women, clad in bright silk gowns and white jackets, kneeling and bowing. Upon the platform we see offerings of rice and flowers, and the air is filled with the perfume of the roses which worshipers have laid at its base. Men are kneeling before it, and as we look boys come up, kneel down, hold up their hands, and pray under the blazing sun.

Let us take a journey up the Irawadi River and see something of the country outside the cities. There are millions of acres of rice farms in Burma. Rangun is the greatest rice port in the world. The valley of the river is made up of rice fields, and we see men here and there plowing. They use wooden plows, and they are doing their work in the laziest way. In some places they do not plow at all, but instead the children drive the water buffaloes and oxen up and down through the mud until the earth has been thoroughly mixed, and then logs are hauled over the fields to smooth them down.

Children from Upper Burma.

The rice plants are first grown in nurseries, just as in Japan, and the women and children set them out in the fields, using their fingers to make the holes in the earth into which they drop the plants. The farmer usually squats on the edge of the field and smokes while the rest of the family work.

After planting, little is done with the rice until harvest. The grain is then cut with sickles, little more than the heads being taken off. It is partly threshed by laying it on a hard place upon the ground and driving bullocks over it. After this it is taken to the river and shipped to Rangun, whence it is sent to all parts of the world.

A grain of rice, when it leaves the farmer, is much like a grain of wheat with the husk on it. This shell or husk must be taken off before the rice is shipped away to other countries, and there are great mills for this purpose, which employ thousands of men. They are not unlike the large flour mills of America.

Let us visit a rice mill and see how the husks are taken off from the little grains without spoiling the rice. The husks stick to the grains as though they were glued, and it is no easy task. We find that the rice must be passed through one pair of millstones after another. These millstones are so carefully set that they tear the husk off without breaking the little white grain which lies within it.

After the husk is removed the grain must be smoothed up for the market. It is queer to think of rice being polished like our best silver spoons, but that is what is done with the rice at Rangun. After the grains are husked they are thrown by machinery against a roller covered with sheepskin as soft as the inside of a kid glove. They are brought into contact with this roller again and again until they are perfectly smooth.

Five hundred miles up the river we reach the city of Mandalay, where the kings of Burma ruled before Great

Britain took possession of the country. In times past, according to a custom in Burma, the location of the capital was changed at the wish of the king, and it was in 1856 that one of the Burmese monarchs decided to move his capital from farther up the river down to Mandalay. The city is now controlled by the British, and the palaces of the king were for a long time used as government offices.

In Mandalay we see people belonging to several of the different tribes which make up the population of interior Burma. We find the Karens', who to a large extent worship good and evil spirits; the Shans, who have curious customs of their own; and a number of hill tribes, who load themselves down with brass jewelry, and are half savage in their ways of living.

We have discovered that Farther India is almost a little world of its own, and we long for the strange things which we are yet to find in India itself. We sail back to Rangun and take a ship for Hindustan. We steam along the eastern coast of the Bay of Bengal, through the muddy waters which lie at its head. We float along the mouths of the Ganges, and cast anchor at last in the Hugli (hoo'gle) River, under the spires and towers of the great city of Calcutta.

Shan Women.

India and Indo-China.

XXIV. GENERAL VIEW OF INDIA.

THE peninsula of Hindustan, or India (without Burma), is almost half as large as the United States. If we could view it all from a balloon we should find that its shape is nearly that of a triangle, the base resting in the Himalaya Mountains, and the sharp southern end lying within a few degrees of the equator. We should see at the north of the peninsula the snow-clad Himalayas, and should notice that its central and southern parts are a vast plateau. Between this plateau and the Himalaya Mountains we might cast our eyes over the wide plains of northern India — plains so low that if you could sink them but a few hundred feet the sea would rush in, and the central and southern parts of Hindustan would be one great island. If our telescope were powerful enough we might see that the country is swarming with people. We might see villages by the thousand and great cities, the names of which we seldom hear.

India contains about two hundred and eighty million people. It has more than one sixth of the population of the world within its boundaries, and upon some parts of it the people are crowded more closely together than upon any other part of the earth.

India is a land of many races. The most of its people, though their skins are dark, have features as regular in their shape as our own, and India is said to have been the cradle of the race from which we sprang.

The people of India are of different religions. The rich island of Ceylon, off the southern end of Hindustan, is one of the centers of the worship of Buddha. There are parts of Hindustan which are populated almost entirely by Mohammedans. It is said that there are more Mohammedans in India than in Turkey, the number of such worshipers being supposed to be more than fifty million. The majority of the people, however, are Hindus, who worship idols of various kinds, and whose religious superstitions we shall notice everywhere as we pass through the country.

The peninsula is divided up into many states, the most of which are governed by Great Britain. Some parts of the country, it is true, are still ruled by rajahs, or native Indian princes, but every such prince has a British adviser at his court, so that the whole of Hindustan is in some way subject to the United Kingdom. Many Englishmen have made great fortunes in India, and their government collects in taxes from it the enormous sum of more than two hundred million dollars a year.

This is a very valuable piece of property, is it not?

And still England got this mighty estate through a pinch of pepper. In the days of Queen Elizabeth, the Dutch controlled the most of the Indian trade. Holland had foreign settlements in India, and one of the chief articles which the Dutch ships carried from there to Europe was pepper, which then sold for seventy-five cents a pound. This gave a large profit to the Dutch merchants, but they were not satisfied, and they doubled the price, making it $1.50 a pound. The English merchants said this was too much, but the Dutch would not put down the price, and so the English formed a company to build ships of their own which should bring pepper and other articles from India to England. This was the famous East India Company, which gradually drove out the most of the Dutch, and from which the British government got possession of the great peninsula.

The chief ruler of India is now a governor general, or viceroy, appointed by the British government. The governor general has a great deal of power. He lives in a fine palace at Calcutta, and has thousands of officials under him. He has control of the armies of India. In all the states there are soldiers, and among them are many natives who ride upon camels and elephants. The soldiers of one such army may be of half a dozen different races. The baggage is carried on donkeys, bullocks, and camels, and when the troops pass from one part of the country to another they form a mighty caravan.

The British have greatly improved India. When they first came into Hindustan the people were almost as backward in civilization as the Chinese. Modern schools and colleges have since been established in many of the cities, and India's exports have increased more than sixty fold. They were not more than five million dollars a year when the English first began to get control of the country, but they now amount to about three hundred million dollars a year.

"who ride upon camels"

Great Britain has introduced its postal and telegraph systems into all parts of India. We find post offices in quite small villages, and in some parts of the country the mail carriers go about upon bicycles to deliver their letters. We shall note a curious thing about the telegraph poles: that they are iron.

Why are they made of iron rather than wood?

It is on account of the white ant, which is found in many parts of Hindustan. These ants eat up anything made of wood, and a swarm of them would chew up a telegraph pole like those used in America in a single night.

But how shall we travel? Shall we take camels or elephants, or shall we have to rely on the rivers as we did in our journey through China?

No. The British have built railroads connecting all the great cities of Hindustan. We can ride over the country almost as rapidly as we travel at home. There are about nineteen thousand miles of railroads in India, the most of which belong to the government. The Indian cars are much like our own, except that the seats are long benches running lengthwise through the cars.

A Native Mail Carrier.

Can we travel at night? Yes, but there are no sleeping cars. We shall have to carry our bedding and rush for the seats, for the man who first gets his bedding down upon a bench has the right to it. If we get there too late we shall be crowded up to the ends of the benches and have to sleep as best we can.

It is only the first- and second-class cars that have what we should call comfortable accommodations. We find the third-class cars reserved for the natives. They pay less than half a cent a mile to ride, but they are packed in so tightly upon the seats that it is almost impossible for them

A Mode of Traveling in India.

to move. The first-class fares are much cheaper than those of our railroads. All the trains have native conductors. Tall, dark-faced men in turbans take up our tickets, and we have some curious experiences with them.

We are amused at the queer things we see on the freight cars. There is one loaded with camels, and there is another in which a little baby elephant is shut off in a pen from the rest of the freight. The conductor tells us that elephant calves are charged for at the rate of six cents a mile, and we wonder what other animals pay.

In the baggage cars we find that there are compartments, or boxes, for cats, monkeys, rabbits, guinea pigs, and dogs. All these animals are classed as dogs, and paid for at the dog rate. No one is allowed to carry any of them into the passenger cars. Not long ago a woman appeared with a turtle in her hand. She was about to enter a car when the Hindu guard stopped her. She asked him why she could not take her pet into the car. He thought for some time and then replied, in his ungrammatical English:

"Yes, Missy can take! Cats is dogs, and monkeys is dogs; but turtles is fish, and there is no rule against fish!"

But here we are in the city of Calcutta! What a curious city it is! Its houses are of stone and brick painted white. They are of two and three stories. They have flat roofs, and doors which open directly out on the street. The streets are wide and well kept, for Calcutta is the capital of India. It is also the largest city of the country, although Bombay, on the other side of the peninsula, is nearly as large, and there are a number of other great business cities.

As we go through Calcutta, we are surrounded with curious sights. Naked babies play in the streets. Men dressed in little more than a long cotton cloth which they have wrapped about their waists go on the trot carrying burdens to and fro. Vehicles such as you will see only in India are driven rapidly this way and that. There are carts drawn by bullocks with humps on their backs. There are cabs known as gharries (găr'rēz) pulled by lean horses and driven by coachmen wearing white gowns and bright-colored turbans. There are carriages drawn by magnificent horses, each with a coachman and footman riding on the box and one or two servants standing on the step behind. The most of these carriages contain Indian princes from neighboring states who are living for the time in the city, or they may be carrying the families of rich British officers.

We see fat Hindu priests known as Brahmans, dressed in white cotton, walking slowly along, and there are Hindu servants in all sorts of costumes running to and fro through the streets.

There comes a Parsee from Bombay! His face is the color of cream, and he wears a brimless hat which looks like an inverted coal scuttle. His coat is much like the frock coat worn in America, but it is buttoned up tight to his throat. The Parsees are merchants, and they are among the richest people of India. They have a curious religion, connected with which is the giving of their bodies to be eaten by vultures after they are dead.

As we go on we see Mohammedans in turbans and gowns. We see black-faced men from south India who wear little more than a piece of white cotton, the size of a sheet, to hide their black skins;—and mixed with all these there are other curious characters, each of whom has a dress of his own, and of whom we shall see more in our tour through the country.

XXV. INDIAN FARMS AND FARMERS.

TO-DAY we leave Calcutta and travel for hundreds of miles along the river Ganges. We are going through the plains of north India, and over some of the richest soil of the world. The sun shines brightly. The crops grow luxuriantly, and birds by the thousand sing in the trees. All nature seems to be joyful, and the only poor thing we can see is man.

There is no land where men struggle so hard and get so little as they do in India. There are parts of the Ganges valley where three hundred and twenty persons get their living out of every one hundred and sixty acres, and where the population is so great that it averages more than twelve hundred to the square mile.

The Hindus are a nation of farmers, the great majority getting their living directly from the soil. In fact, India has many more farmers than we have men, women, and children in the United States. The farmers raise all kinds of crops. They grow wheat which competes with ours in the markets of Europe. Their cotton is mixed with that from our Southern States in many of the great factories of the world, and they raise quantities of coffee, spices, indigo, and opium.

You would naturally think such people would be rich. We find them terribly poor. The clothing of the men, as they work in the fields, is little more than a strip of white cotton five yards long which they wrap about their bodies and pull between their legs, fastening the end at the waist. In addition to this many wear cotton jackets, and sometimes an additional strip of cloth which they wind about their shoulders. Both men and women look as though they had taken the sheets from their beds to wrap about them as clothing. A woman usually holds the sheet over her face to hide it from the men, leaving only a crack through which we see one of her black eyes looking out. The women sometimes have little sleeveless jackets of cotton which reach just below the armpits, and under which there is a skirt which falls to their ankles.

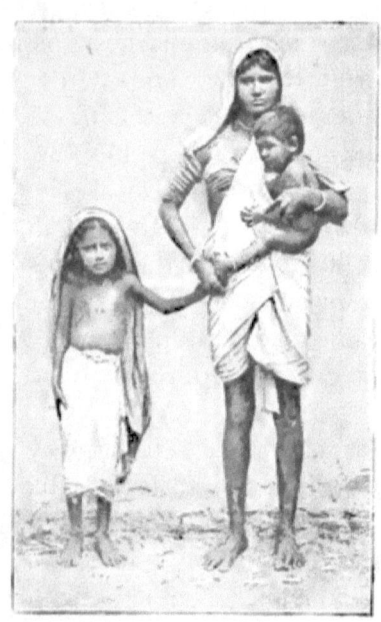

Peasant Woman and Children

Almost all of the people go barefooted. The men are barelegged, and as we look we see that the working people of north India are little more than skin and bone. During our travels through the plains of the Ganges we shall probably not see a man who has calves on his legs as big as the muscles of the upper arm of a healthy sixteen-year-old American boy. The women are equally lean, and we can count the ribs of many of the babies, who are usually naked.

The poor people in this part of Hindustan eat just enough to keep them alive, and it is said that there are millions who do not know what it is to go to bed without being hungry. Their food is rice or millet, and their drink is water. In the opium districts we are told that the farmers sometimes feed their children opium to take away their hunger and to keep them from feeling the cold. Millions of men in India support their families on an income of fifty cents a week, and we see women who are working in the fields for about three cents a day.

The farmers of India do not live upon their farms. They cluster together like bees in little villages of mud huts. These villages have no modern improvements whatever. The average hut is fifteen or sixteen feet

Fuel Gatherers.

square. It has an almost flat roof made of thin earthen tiles, or of straw thatch. It has no chimney, and the smoke finds its way out through the door or from under the eaves. Well-to-do farmers may have several huts with a mud wall around them.

Upon the walls of most of the huts are plastered lumps of brown mud about the size and shape of a fat buckwheat cake. We see tens of thousands of these cakes in every town. In some villages they cover the sides of the huts, and here and there we come upon great piles of them which have been dried and stacked up for sale. These mud cakes form the fuel of a great part of India. They are made of manure and earth mixed together. Timber is very scarce on the plains of Hindustan, and the cooking is all done over fires of this dry manure. It is gathered up every day by the women and girls from the roads and fields, so that not a bit goes to waste.

But let us look inside the house of an Indian farmer. The floor is of mud and the walls are unplastered. How uncomfortable it is! There are neither tables nor chairs, and the family squat on the ground at their meals.

Where is the bed? It has been put outside of the hut in order that the family may have more room. It is merely a network of ropes stretched on a framework of wood, with legs at the corners. It is only about four feet long and three feet wide, and the Hindu sleeps upon it with his legs doubled up. If he stretched them out they would hang over the end of the bed.

Sometimes the men sleep outside the houses. The East Indians of the poorer classes do not use nightgowns or nightshirts, and in our walks through the towns in the early morning we see very few bedclothes, either under or over the black forms which lie upon these networks of rope.

What are those curtains hung up in front of the doors of many of the huts? They are to keep the men from seeing the women who are within. The women of the upper classes live in the back huts, or back rooms, for many women are secluded in India, and are never seen by any other men than those of their own family.

FARMS AND FARMERS.

The farming tools are of the rudest description. The Hindu plow is little more than a sharpened stick. It is so light that the farmer carries it to and from the fields on his shoulders. The furrows are mere scratches on the surface of the ground, but the fields are gone over so often that the soil is ground to dust and is made to produce very large crops.

We see men doing everything by hand. There the people are cutting the grain with sickles. The wheat is sometimes pulled from the ground, the straw being saved to feed the cattle.

Plowing.

Outside some of the huts we find women at work making the meal or flour for the family. They pour the grain through a hole in one large round stone which rests upon another, and then turn the top stone around until the wheat or millet is thoroughly ground.

The wheat-growing districts of India are in the north. The British government is doing all that it can to increase the production of wheat, and it is said that the area of Indian wheat farms is now about two thirds as large as that of the wheat farms in the United States. The government has constructed great irrigation works in order to make the country as far as possible independent of rain. The rivers of India bring down from the mountains every year vast quantities of rich fertilizing material, and wher-

" — and then turn the top stone around — "

ever their waters can be spread over the land they give the benefit of both the moisture and the manure.

The people of India can raise wheat more cheaply than we can. They spend but little for machinery. The wheat is threshed by being trodden out by bullocks and buffaloes. They have no barns, and they pile the wheat up on the ground until it is shipped to the markets. Men can be hired to do farm work for from six to eight cents a day, and it costs the farmers but little to live.

One of the most curious of the Indian crops is indigo. Hundreds of thousands of acres are devoted to it in Hindustan. Indigo comes from a plant which grows to a height of from three to five feet. When the plants are ready to flower they are cut off close to the ground, tied up in small bundles, and put into large vats of water. In about ten hours they begin to ferment, and the water becomes yellow. It is then run off into other vats, in which half-naked men stand and whip the fluid with long bamboo sticks, keeping it constantly in motion for two or three hours.

After a while the liquor turns from yellow to green, and the blue particles of indigo rise in flakes, which afterward sink to the bottom of the vat. The liquor is then allowed to settle, and the sediment, or that which goes to the bottom, is indigo. The water is drawn off, and the indigo is boiled and pressed into cakes to be shipped to different parts of the world for use in washing clothes, making paints, and for other purposes.

We have beautiful poppies in our flower beds in America. India has vast fields of poppies, and we travel for miles through them on our way over the country. The Indian poppies are not for show, however. They are raised for the making of opium. The British government controls the entire crop and receives many millions of dollars every year from the sale of opium. Every Indian farmer who plants poppies must first get the permission of the British officials and agree to sell to the government all the opium he produces.

The poppy seeds are sown in November, and the plants are plowed and weeded from that time until about February, when they burst out into white flowers. When the flowers have become full-grown and are just ready to drop off, the pods are cut or scratched with a thin piece of iron. This is done in the evening. In the morning the poppy juice which has oozed out on the pod is scraped off, and this juice is opium. When it first comes from the pod it is of a milky-white color, but it gradually changes to a rose red.

It takes a great many plants to make much opium. The farmer rubs the scrapings of each plant oft into the palm of his left hand until he has collected several ounces, when he puts them into an earthen jar. When he has gathered his whole crop he turns the jars over to the government and receives the regular price for it.

The government officials take the jars, and from their contents manufacture the opium of commerce, which is shipped to all parts of the world. The most of it goes to China, although some comes to the United States.

Opium is of great value as a medicine. The effect of the frequent use of it, however, is much like that of whisky or brandy. Those who eat or smoke much opium soon find that they cannot get along without it. They become opium drunkards, and it destroys their bodies and minds.

Another plant which is of great value to the world is raised in large quantities in many parts of India. This is the flax plant, from the fibers of which linen cloth is made, and from which comes the strongest of our sewing thread. There are many thousands of acres of flax plants in India, but they are not raised there for the fibers. The flaxseed is very valuable. The plants, after growing to the height of about three feet, burst out into beautiful blue flowers, and later on little balls of flaxseed take the places of these flowers. Each tiny ball contains ten seeds.

The seeds are flat, oval, and dark brown in color. They shine as though they were varnished. Their kernels are very oily, and when pressed they yield the linseed oil of commerce. This is used for making paints, oilcloth, and other things.

A great part of the linseed oil used by our painters comes from India. Is it not strange to think that the houses in which we live are painted with oil made by these curious people so many thousand miles away on the other side of the globe?

One of the most important of the Indian fiber plants is that from which jute is made. During our tour through Japan we saw beautiful Japanese rugs woven from jute. This material is also used for the making of rope, bagging and other coarse cloth.

The jute plant is a sort of reed which grows in the low, sandy soil along the banks of the Indian rivers. The seed is sown in April and the crop becomes ripe in August. The plants grow to the height of twelve feet, or twice the height of a man. When ripe they are cut off close to the ground and are thrown into water in order that the outer skin or bark may be rotted. After a short time this skin becomes so soft that it can be peeled off, and the fiber or wood within can be taken out and washed. This fiber is made up of long, silky strands which can easily be made into thread. The fiber needs little preparation for the market, for after washing it is put up in bales, and is then ready for shipment to other parts of the world.

A great deal of cotton is raised in India, and we shall find large cotton factories in some of the cities.

XXVI. THE STORES AND TRADES OF INDIA.

THE business of the cities of India is done in bazaars much like those which we visited at Rangun, in Burma. We find hundreds of little stores under one roof. Each store is not much bigger than a dry-goods box, and the dark-faced merchant within it squats on the floor with his goods piled around him.

There are streets lined with shops, each about as large

as a good-sized closet, in which all kinds of manufacturing go on. Such establishments are open during the day. Their fronts are removed, and we can see men of all trades at their work. We pass through streets walled with shoe shops. The shoemakers sit flat on the floor. They are

A Business Street in India.

all barefooted, and they hold the leather between their toes while they sew. The carpenters also use their feet in holding their work, and they saw while squatting down on the floor.

We see little shops not more than six feet in width, in which men are sitting and making wire of gold or silver. The strands are so fine that at first we think the wire is

Women Weaving in India.

silk thread, and cannot believe that it is made of metal. Our guide asks us for a coin, and tells us that he will have it turned into wire. We give him an American twenty-five-cent piece. He hands it over to one of the black-faced workmen, and within a short time it has been made into a silver wire almost half a mile long. There are a thousand men engaged in wiredrawing in the city of Lucknow, and in Delhi we see dark-faced Hindu men and boys using the wire to embroider ladies' dresses which are to be sent to Europe for sale.

The Indians make most beautiful embroideries, and their embroidered curtains are among the finest of the world. Think of cloth so expensive that enough of it for a lady's dress costs from two hundred to five thousand dollars! This is the famous kincob cloth which is woven at Ahmadabad, in north India. It is a heavy brocade of gold and silver, and it is, perhaps, the most costly cloth made anywhere.

A Hindu Carpenter.

Let us take a look at some Indian shawls. The cashmere shawls are made of the fine wool of the cashmere goat. The weaving is done by families who work at the trade from one generation to another. We find the shawls very expensive; some cost two hundred dollars and upwards, according to size.

Our Hindu merchant has other shawls of all kinds and prices. He hands us one and asks us to lift it. It is very light. He then takes it, and with the aid of his clerks opens it out. It is as large as a bedquilt. He asks us for a ring. I pull one from my little finger and hand it to him, when, lo, he puts one end of the shawl into the ring and draws the whole shawl through it. This is the famous ring shawl of India, one of the softest and finest of all woolen fabrics.

A Shawl Merchant.

As we go through the business parts of the Indian cities, we are surprised to see how anxious every one is to sell. Some of the dealers stand at the doors of their stores, and put their hands together and beseech us to buy. They can speak only a few words of English, but they cry out, "Me poor man, Sahib! Me good man! Sahib buy something!"

No matter how fast we go, the peddlers run along by our carriages and try to thrust their wares in upon us.

We find that nearly every important merchant has men about the hotels who ask foreigners to come to his shop to trade. Such men are to be seen also about the bazaars. They jump upon the steps of our carriages and beg us to go to their masters' shops. They all say that their places are the cheapest, but we know that if we go with them they will get a commission or a part of all the money we spend.

"It is made of the purest white marble."

There are many such men connected with the jewelry shops, and we soon learn that the making of jewelry is one of the great industries of north Hindustan. The Hindus have been noted for ages for their fine work in gold, silver, and precious stones. At Agra, in north India, stands the Taj Mahal, which is thought by travelers to be the most beautiful building of the whole world. It is made of the purest white marble. When it was completed its interior was largely inlaid with jewels and precious stones. It was constructed by Shah Jehan, a Mohammedan ruler of northern India, as a tomb for his favorite wife.

Shah Jehan was the ruler who owned the famous peacock throne. This throne was made in the form of a peacock, the feathers of which were of precious stones in the natural colors of the peacock's tail. Diamonds, rubies, carbuncles, emeralds, and many other kinds of jewels were gathered together from everywhere for it, and it was of such value that it cost, it is said, the enormous sum of thirty million dollars.

We have heard of these wonderful jewels of India's past, and we see that the women almost everywhere are loaded down with necklaces, bracelets, and rings; so we ask to be taken to the jewelry shops. We think of the fine stores of our American cities, and a vision of plate-glass cases and of a gorgeous display of watches and rings comes before our minds.

What do we find?

The store which we first visit is little more than a hole in the wall. It is about ten feet square, and is entirely open to the street. The owner of the store, who is dressed in a long gown, does not look very rich, and we think our guide has made a mistake.

The merchant, however, asks us to come in, and offers us a seat on the floor. He directs a servant to bring a red cashmere shawl, and spreads this out between us and him. He gives another direction, and the servant goes over to the corner of the room and brings back a bundle. It looks like a lot of old clothes wrapped up in a dirty white cotton cloth.

The bundle is placed in front of the merchant. He opens it and spreads out before our eyes a stock of gold and silver jewelry, of diamonds, rubies, sapphires, and pearls which dazzle our eyes. Upon the red shawl he lays bracelets and strings of pearls, rubies, and sapphires. Beside them he places a necklace of diamonds, each of which is as big as a good-sized bean, and to these adds strands of topazes and emeralds, hanging one by the other from a great gold band, or set in curiously carved gold. There are rings of all prices. There are brooches of many kinds, and we almost gasp as we see the fortune before us.

We pick out a ring and bargain an hour before we can buy. In India there are no fixed prices, and it is usual to bargain in making a purchase. We cannot get accustomed to this method of buying, and we soon learn that it is best to say just how much we will give, and then walk away. We seldom go more than a few steps before the Hindu comes running after us with the goods, and grudgingly tells us that we can have them at our own price. The Hindu has more time than money, and he will talk all day for a very few cents.

On our way back to the hotel we are stopped by a wedding procession. We are surprised to learn that the groom is a boy of fifteen, and that the bride is only eight years of age. The groom has a red cloth cap on his head, and is dressed in tawdry red clothes. He is riding a white pony, and with him is a crowd of barelegged men and boys, his relatives and friends, who trot along on foot as an escort.

The little bride follows behind, but we cannot see her, for she is shut up in what looks like a large trunk covered with red cloth. The box is hung upon a pole which is carried on the shoulders of men. Behind come a number of women who are bringing the bride's property or dower. One group carries her bed. Another holds up a tray upon which are her cooking utensils, consisting of three or four iron pots and a rice jar, which altogether would not be worth more than $1.50 of our money. We learn that the bride and groom will not live together until the girl is about twelve years of age, when she will come from her parents' home to that of her husband's and be married for good.

Thousands of girls are married every year in India while they are still babies. Such wives do not live with their husbands until they have reached the age of ten or twelve years. If in the mean time the husband should die, the fate of the child wife is terrible.

Hindu widows cannot marry again, and are despised by their families and every one else. A widow usually lives in the house of her mother-in-law, and the members of the family do all they can to make her life miserable, for it is supposed that the husband is happy in heaven just in proportion as his widow is unhappy on earth. She cannot go to parties. She must eat by herself, and must cook her own food apart from the family.

The women of India are in fact the slaves of their husbands. They receive but little education, and they have but few rights. The Hindu wife never eats until her husband gets through, and she takes what is left. The poorer women do the hardest kind of work. We see them digging in the fields, breaking stone upon the roads, and carrying great burdens upon their heads.

Such hardships prevail among nearly all the women of India, with the exception of the Parsees. The Parsees are a small colony of people who live in west Hindustan, the most of them having their homes in Bombay. They are of Persian descent, and they have a religion and life of their own. Parsee children are never married under

A Parsee Family.

twelve. The women are not secluded, and they can go about wherever they please. The Parsees are, as a rule, good business men. They are very intelligent, and many of them are rich.

XXVII. THE WILD ANIMALS OF INDIA.

YOU would not think that a country so thickly populated as India could have many wild animals. The peninsula of Hindustan, however, has vast jungles composed of forest trees, thickets of bamboo, creeping vines, and growths of underbrush of that dense kind which is found only in tropical countries. The jungles cover the lower slopes of the Himalaya Mountains for many miles just back of the rich plains of north India, and they are to be found here and there upon the high plateaus of central and southern India.

In the jungles fierce tigers roam, panthers have their lairs, and jackals, hyenas, and wolves make night hideous with their cries. The wild beasts dash out now and then into the farming districts and kill men, women, and children. It is estimated that three thousand persons are eaten every year by wild animals in India, and that more than nineteen thousand are killed by poisonous snakes. About one thousand people are eaten every year by tigers alone, and in a single year sixty-one thousand cattle perished from the attacks of wild beasts.

The wild animals of India are of many curious kinds. There are wild dogs in Assam, on the edge of the Himalaya Mountains, which always hunt in packs. Twenty-five or thirty of these dogs go together, and when once a pack of them is on the track of an animal, no matter whether it is a deer or a tiger, that animal is sure to die. They will follow it for days. If it comes to bay they will attack it at once, and if it runs they will pursue it until it becomes tired out and falls.

The rhinoceroses which are found in the swamps of the Brahmaputra valley often grow to be six feet in height, and the great horns above their noses sometimes attain a length of more than a foot. There are crocodiles from eighteen to twenty feet long in many of the Indian rivers, and there are wild elephants in some parts of the country.

The hunting of elephants is now entirely under government control. It is against the law to shoot them, and whoever captures or injures an elephant in India without a license will be fined an amount equal to one hundred dollars and put into prison. Elephants are caught by driving them into stockades or great pens which are made in the forests. The process is very dangerous, for if an angry elephant can get at a hunter he will jump upon the man and crush him. When the hunter falls to the ground the elephant kicks him backward and forward between his fore and

Rhinoceros.

hind feet, and sometimes, it is said, by means of his trunk and his feet tears the body limb from limb.

Jackals abound everywhere throughout India, and we often hear their yells, which sound somewhat like those of a screaming baby, or of a man in anguish. Jackals look like very large foxes. They have jaws so strong that they can crush bones between their teeth. They are sneaking, cowardly animals, who will put their tails between their legs and run away at the sight of a man, though they sometimes attack children and infirm old people.

The tiger is said to reach its greatest size in the jungles of India, though there are enormous tigers in Manchuria and Korea. I once saw a dozen of the largest Bengal tigers in the Zoölogical Garden at Calcutta. One of them which measured almost twelve feet from nose to tail was being fed at the time. Some meat had been put inside the

Tiger.

door of his cage. The keeper had gone away, and the great beast was devouring the flesh, when I poked my umbrella through the bars as though to touch the meat. At this the mighty tiger raised his head and sprang at the iron bars with a terrific roar. My heart sank, and I started to run. As I did so the keeper came and told me to be very careful of that tiger, as he was a man-eater and had already killed one hundred people.

It is said that when a tiger has once tasted human flesh he prefers it to all other food; and it seemed to me that the tigers I saw in India devoured me with their eyes, licking their lips as they looked, and possibly wondering how good American flesh would taste. A single tiger is known to have killed 108 people in three years. Another is said to have killed on an average 80 persons a year, and a third, only a few years ago, killed 127 people. It prowled along one of the public roads of India for many weeks, stopping all traffic, until an English sportsman came along and killed it.

The tiger usually does his hunting at night. He often has his lair in a jungle near a village, or near the fields where the cattle are kept. After dark he creeps out until he is within a few feet of his victim, and then with a spring seizes it by the throat, often twisting it about so as to dislocate its neck. In the case of human beings, an old man-eater will sometimes grab a person by the shoulders with his teeth, swing the body about over his back, and trot off with his living victim into the jungle to devour him at leisure.

The tiger is very strong. He can strike down a cow with a blow of one of his paws, and can drag it off with his teeth. His claws are as white as ivory, and almost as hard as steel. They can be covered at will, like those of a cat, and they are drawn in by the tiger while he is walking, so that they are not worn and blunted by being rubbed against the ground.

Tigers are not brave animals, and, with the exception of those who have tasted human flesh, they will run from man rather than face him. When hunted, however, they fight to desperation. Elephants are much used by the tiger hunters, and a tiger often springs on the back of the elephant, or jumps up on his head, in the attempt to get at the men who are riding him.

These fierce beasts are sometimes caught in pits and traps, and the hunters often make a little platform in a tree near where a tiger comes to eat or drink, and there watch for him with their guns loaded. A young buffalo or a calf is usually tied near the foot of the tree, and when the tiger has sprung upon the animal the hunters shoot him.

Hindus are very much afraid of the tiger, and the people often leave a village after it has been attacked once or twice by these beasts. A single tiger sometimes drives away a large number of people, visiting a town night after night and taking off a man or a baby at each visit.

We shall be in more danger, however, from snakes than from tigers in our travels in this part of the world. India has some of the most poisonous snakes known to man. They are often found in the gardens. They live in the roofs of some of the houses, and we shall not dare to walk through the fields without watching.

One of the most dangerous of all snakes is the cobra. It is not a large snake, being seldom more than four or five feet long, though it sometimes grows to a length of six feet and to a thickness of six inches. The cobra has a small head, which it expands into the shape of a hood when it is angry. It rises on its tail when it strikes. Its bite is almost sure death, few persons ever recovering from it. The cobra cannot move very fast, and cannot, it is said, strike a distance greater than its own length.

An English lady describes a curious experience that she had with a cobra. She was writing one day at her desk in her Indian home to her friends in England, when all at once she felt as though somebody was looking at her from behind. She glanced around twice, but could see nothing. At last, on the floor, she saw a cobra raising its hood-shaped head and just about to spring at her. She jumped upon the table and screamed for her servants, who rushed in and killed the snake.

Many of the Hindu jugglers are also snake tamers, and they are among the most skillful of their kind in the world.

Snake Charmers.

We shall meet them in all of the cities. Each wears a couple of pieces of dirty white cotton, one of which he winds around his waist, and the other over his shoulders. His arms are bare to the elbows, and his clothes are so scanty that it would seem impossible to conceal anything in them.

I remember how a snake charmer once frightened me at Delhi. He asked me to hold out my hand, and he then placed a piece of brown paper upon it. He next took up a flute and began to play, looking at the paper and darting out his eyes as though he saw something there. He danced around me for some time, playing all the while, and keeping his weird black eyes upon my hand. Then he started back and looked at the paper. I also looked, but could see nothing. He did this again and again, dancing about more wildly than ever. At last he dropped the flute and commenced to sing, continuing his dance and pointing again and again at the paper upon my hand.

All at once, while I was looking at the paper and seeing nothing, he thrust out his naked arm, and clapped his bare hand down upon the paper, and snatched out of my very hand, it seemed to me, three great cobras. He held them up before my frightened eyes, and the snakes raised their hooded heads and darted out their fangs at me, and squirmed and wriggled as he held them. I jumped back, for the cobras were within a few inches of my nose. I could not tell then, and I do not know now, where the snakes came from. I saw the trick again and again, but I could never discover how it was done.

It is said by some that the jugglers pull out the fangs of the snakes; but this is not true in all cases. A short time ago an Englishman at Benares accused a juggler of doing this. He said that he was not afraid to handle the cobras, for he knew that they could not hurt him. The juggler protested, and warned the man that the snakes were dangerous. The Englishman thought they were not, and seized one of them. It bit him in the arm, and within a few hours he died.

A juggler's outfit usually consists of three baskets, ranging in size from a half peck to a bushel, a couple of cloths, a little string, and some sticks. He has three little wooden dolls with red cloths tied around their necks, and he says that these are the gods which help him in his magic. He sometimes has a monkey's skull which he moves to and fro over the articles he is using, as though calling the spirit of the monkey to his aid. Another assistant in some cases is a little black boy whose clothing is a turban, or cap, and a cloth about his waist.

With this boy the juggler performs the wonderful basket trick of India, which has become famous all over the world. The boy's hands are tied and he is put into a net, which is drawn over his head and which incloses his whole body so that he does not seem to be able to move. The net is tied after being put on. The boy is now placed in a basket about two feet square, or just about the size of a large clothes basket. This basket has a lid, which is pulled down and fastened with straps running around it and buckled tightly over it.

The juggler now takes a long, sharp sword, and then, after moving the monkey's skull over the basket, and shaking his little doll babies, thrusts his sword again and again into and through the basket. There is a crying, as though some one was in terrible pain. It is the voice of a child, and the sword comes out bloody. You hold your breath, and if you did not know it to be a trick you would feel like pouncing upon the man. After a few moments the basket becomes still. The juggler sticks his bloody sword into it a few more times, and then unbuckles the strap and opens it. The basket is empty. The boy has disappeared. The man then cries out "Baba, baba," and in the distance you hear the voice of the child, who soon comes up unhurt. How the boy gets out of the basket or escapes being killed by the sword you cannot tell; you only know that it is a sleight-of-hand performance, and wonderfully well done.

XXVIII. BENARES, THE HOLY CITY OF THE HINDUS.

WE must take an early start for our travels to-day. We are going to visit Benares. It is the holiest of all the cities of Hindustan. The Hindu who dies within ten miles of it feels sure of going to a better life, and if he can bathe in the Ganges where it flows by Benares he thinks that all his sins will be washed off forever. The Ganges River is holy throughout its entire length, but at Benares is the holiest part, though there is another holy place not far away, at Allahabad. Some people believe that if a man's head is shaved at Allahabad, he will receive a million years in paradise for each hair which falls into the water.

Bathing in the Ganges.

Benares contains about two hundred thousand people, and pilgrims go there in crowds from all parts of India, some walking for hundreds of miles, that they may pray and bathe in the Ganges. There are thousands who have moved to Benares to die, and we shall find great numbers in the temples.

There are more than one thousand temples in Benares.

They line the banks of the Ganges for miles, and by taking a boat and floating by them we can see one of the most curious sights of the world.

We start for the river not long after daybreak. The roads leading to the temples are already filled with thousands of dark-skinned men and women clad in long strips of cotton, colored white, red, and blue. They wrap the cloths about their bodies, and pull them over their faces, so that their mouths and nostrils are covered, and only their eyes shine out. The air near the river is cold and damp, and is not good to breathe at this time of the morning.

The people are of all classes. The legs of some of them are bare to the knees, and only the richer people wear shoes. Some of them have cashmere shawls of bright red. All

"— gorgeous in jewelry"

the women are gorgeous in jewelry, and even the poorest have their arms covered with silver or brass bracelets from their wrists to their elbows. Upon the ankles of all are silver or gold bands, while not a few have rings and bells on their toes. Many of them have little rings in their noses, and we see some nose rings which are as big round as the bottom of a tin cup. Others have earrings hung from holes running around the outer edge of the ears from the lobes to the tips. All carry brass jars of different sizes and shapes to bring the holy water of the Ganges up to the temples, or back with them to their homes.

We push our way through the crowds, and at the upper end of the city we get a boat in which to float down the

Temple on the Ganges.

river. We have six dusky men, clad in white gowns and high turbans, to row us, and we direct them to keep near the shore. We float along not far from the steps leading from the river up to the temples which line the right bank of the Ganges. There are about three miles of these steps, and upon them thousands of half-naked men, women, and children continually pass up and down.

It is a wonderful sight.

Hundreds are bathing, standing in the Ganges with the water up to their waists. Here and there ledges jut out from the steps, and on them sit worshipers muttering prayers as they lift up the sacred liquid in their brass bowls, and pour it over their bodies. The women are bathing as well as the men. They cluster together in groups by themselves, trying to keep their faces covered so that the men may not see them as they splash about in the water.

As we float onward the sun rises. Its rays make the wet skins of the half-naked men and women shine like polished mahogany. The brass jars look like gold, and the jewelry which the Hindu women wear becomes more gorgeous than ever in the sunlight. A confused noise of prayers and gossip comes to our ears, and we sit and wonder at this worship of the waters of a river, which is real worship to millions of people.

We reach over the edge of the boat, and put our hands down into the water. It is cold, and we wonder at the invalids whom we see among the bathers. Lean, sickly people stand and shiver as they pour the cold water over their bodies. Many are brought here to end their lives, because they think that if they die in the holy Ganges their life in the next world will be happy.

Among the bathers there are many gray-haired men and women. As we look, a skeletonlike old man stands upon the steps of one of the temples, with nothing on but a waistcloth which is glued, as it were, by the water to his dripping skin. He throws upward his shriveled arms, with his long, snaky fingers outstretched, and through chattering teeth prays to the sun.

Just beyond him is a woman who is casting flowers into

the river by way of worship. All about us, on the dryer parts of the steps, under great umbrellas, sit black-skinned priests with little boxes of red and white paint before them, to mark the bathers, as they come out of the water, with the emblems of the heathen gods.

Our boat goes onward. We see smoke rising from the banks between two temples, and we row down to the place. The smoke comes from fires built in the hollow, a little back from the water, where the people are burning their dead.

The Hindus believe in cremation. Every Hindu would like to have his body burned on the banks of the Ganges; for after the burning the ashes are thrown into the holy river, and the souls of the bodies so disposed of are thought to go straight to the better land. The burning of bodies is done everywhere throughout India, and we find cremation places in all the cities.

The temples of Benares are of many kinds. India is a land of many religions. It is a country where religion enters more into the life and business of the people than in any other part of the world. A man's social rank is largely fixed by religion. The people are divided up into classes or castes. Men of each caste carry on the same business, from father to son, and it is a part of the religion that no man shall do any work not belonging to his caste.

In parts of India the people worship stones. Some hill tribes worship spirits who, they think, live in certain trees.

Two of the most famous gods of the Hindus are Siva and Vishnu. Siva is represented as wearing a necklace of skulls and a collar of twining serpents. He has five faces and four arms, and holds a club with a human head on the end of it. Siva's wife is the goddess who presides over all ills, suffering, and death. She is generally represented as riding on a tiger, and sometimes she takes the form of Kali (kä'lē), a woman with a hideous face, whose head is crowned with snakes and hung around with skulls.

One of the most famous temples of Benares is the Monkey Temple. Monkeys are sacred to one of the Hindu gods. We find hundreds of them in the temple. Sleek and fat, they climb the trees that surround it. They scamper through the building and chatter at us as we come in. We have brought some nuts with us. We throw them into the air, and the monkeys catch them as they fall, and grin at us between the bites as they eat them.

You have all heard of the sacred cow of India. It is a beautiful beast. It differs from the ordinary cow in having a great hump just over the shoulders. The Hindus worship such cows. They never kill one, and a Hindu would as soon think of eating his grandfather as of eating a piece of beef.

In Benares we find an immense temple devoted to the worship of cows and bulls. The people think this temple too holy to allow us to enter by the front door, but our guide takes us in through a door at the back. We enter a stone court of about the size of the ordinary barnyard. We think of a barnyard as we look about us. The court is walled with about one hundred stalls, in which there are a hundred sacred bulls with big humps on their backs and with ears which hang down like those of a rabbit, instead of being almost erect like the ears of our cattle. Some are white, some yellow, and some dove-colored.

Here and there through the courtyard a harmless bull moves. The sloppy, dirty stone floor is filled with barefooted Hindus dressed in bright colors. Many of them have brought water from the Ganges in their brass jars. They give this to the bulls, and stand around chanting prayers as the animals drink. Other worshipers are bringing food. We see pretty girls carrying garlands of flowers into the temple. They have red cashmere shawls about their heads, and these they hold over their faces, but we can see their black eyes peeping out in front through the folds. They feed the flowers to the bulls, and pray as the animals lazily chew at the queer food.

Upon a platform in the center of the courtyard are several priests who sit crosslegged, with boxes of paint beside them. As the people finish their prayers, they come to the priests and pay money, whereupon each gets a dab of red or white paint on the forehead. These paint marks are the emblems of certain of the Hindu gods, and everywhere in our travels we meet people so spotted with red and white paint.

"They are used for driving —"

On our way back to the hotel we see many sacred bulls and cows working, and we learn that the people use them for all sorts of hard labor. They pull the plows, and in some parts act as pack animals. They are used for driving, and we pass the carts of rich Hindus, whose bulls wear gorgeous blankets and have their horns decorated with ribbons and flowers.

XXIX. THE NATIVE STATES OF INDIA; OR, A VISIT TO THE RAJAH OF JAIPUR.

A PART of our journey to-day will be upon elephants. We are going to visit the rajah of one of the native states of Hindustan. The whole of India, as we have already learned, is not ruled by Great Britain. There are native states which are governed by rajahs,

A State Elephant.

or Hindu princes. These rulers have gorgeous palaces. They have thousands of servants. Some of them have armies of their own, with camel and elephant troops, and they ride about upon elephants when they go in state from one place to another. They are, to a certain extent, subordinate to the British officials, but they govern their states much as they please.

One of the most famous of the native rulers is the Nizam of Haidarabād, who lives in south-central India, and who governs a country as large as Kansas. His capital city contains more than four hundred thousand people, and his subjects number more than eleven million.

Another great native ruler is the Rajah of Jaipur. He lives in the western part of Hindustan, more than a day's ride by railroad northward from Bombay.

His capital is said to be the finest native city of India, and it is like no other in the world. Imagine a city as large as Omaha made up of beautiful two-story buildings, all of which are painted a delicate rose pink. Let the houses come close to the sidewalk and have balconies hanging over it. Let arcades run below from house to

A Street in Jaipur.

house, so that you can keep out of the sun as you go along the street. Let the streets be laid out regularly, crossing one another at right angles, and let them be as hard and as well made as the roads of any city of the United States. Put a great wall twenty feet high around this city, and let rugged hills rise at its back so that they inclose it in a basin; and you have some idea of the rose-colored city of Jaipur.

We must add, however, to these miles of pink houses the curious sights and the strange people of a rich native Indian city. We must fill the balconies with dark-faced men and boys wearing turbans and gowns, and Hindu maidens with their faces covered with shawls and their eyes shining out through the folds.

Below, opening on the arcades, are shops in which Hindu merchants squat crosslegged with goods piled around them, and sell the countless knickknacks and other things used by the people. Out in the street is one of the most picturesque crowds of men and beasts to be found in the world. There are dark-faced men and women, some rushing here and there, some moving along leisurely, some chatting, and others pushing and yelling.

There are hundreds of camels stalking along through the crowd. Here is one ridden by a woman. She sits astride of the hump. Her bare feet, resting against the animal's sides, show out below golden anklets, and one of her black eyes peeps out of the shawl around her head as she directs the driver, who is leading the beast, where to go.

There is a camel carrying stones. Immense paving flags as big as the top of a table are swung by ropes on both sides of his hump, and he goes along with his lower lip down, pouting like a spoiled child. At the side of the road is another camel being loaded with lumber. The men are tying long rafters, one after another, to his back, and at each addition to his load he blubbers and cries like a baby; and you can see the tears rolling down from his proud, angry eyes. Here is a camel ridden by a turbaned soldier, and behind him trots another with a boy on his back.

There come some elephants. There are a dozen of them, each ridden by a black driver who wears a white turban.

These elephants belong to the rajah, and the servants are giving them their daily exercise.

There are thousands of bullocks carrying hay, stone, and merchandise through the city. Here comes a sacred bull with a man on his back. The rider wears a turban, and his long beard, fine gown, and red shoes turned up at the toes attract our attention as he goes by.

Then there are beautiful Arabian horses ridden by the rich men of the city and by the rajah's officials. Some of the riders have gold chains on their necks, and their arms and fingers are heavy with gold. They wear gold-embroidered turbans and costly gold vests, and their legs are covered with rich cloths. They sit up straight as they ride, and by the side of each runs a groom, now clearing the way for his master, and now running along by his stirrup, waiting for orders.

The crowd on foot is as gay as that riding upon animals. Here comes a party of Hindu singing girls, who shout out strange songs as they dance through the streets. They are dark-faced, but by no means bad-looking. Their forms are draped in gay-colored cloths, and their limbs are loaded with anklets. Behind them walk some Mohammedan women, whose dresses make them seem hideous to us. Each wears a short jacket and a divided skirt of red or purple cotton which is full at the waist, but which fits close to the skin below the knees.

What queer sights are these we see on the streets! Look at those women breaking stones at the side of the road! They are clad in garments of dirty white cotton, but, poor as they are, they have great silver rings on their ankles, and bracelets of silver or glass on their wrists. We see women and girls with rings in their noses, and there are many girls with rings on their toes.

Here comes the street-sprinkling machine of Jaipur. It is that brown-skinned, half-naked man with that bag on his back. The bag is made of a pigskin, and it holds several gallons of water. We have seen men like him in all the Indian cities. They are water carriers, and the business descends from father to son. They scatter the water over the street by holding the hand over the mouth of the bag and swinging themselves this way and that as they walk.

Passing through scenes of this kind, we come at last to the rajah's palace. It consists of several large buildings surrounding courts paved with marble. It contains many rooms which are carpeted with magnificent rugs, and the floor of one great hall is covered with hundreds of skins of tigers and leopards, the hunting trophies of the rajah.

"— the street-sprinkling machine

But we are to have an elephant ride. The rajah has ordered that his best elephants be brought out for us. We are going to spend a day in a jaunt through the country. We have not much time to stay in the palace, and we ask to be shown to the stables.

We find that the elephants are being made ready for us. What magnificent creatures they are! They are larger than any elephants we have yet seen. They have great brass chains about their necks, and their white tusks — which are cut off halfway up from the end — are bound with heavy brass rings.

The keepers lead them out into the courtyard, and Hindu elephant drivers make them kneel down in order

" — we have to mount them by ladders."

that they may be saddled, and that we may climb on their backs. The saddle is an immense framework cushioned with cloth. The beasts are so large that even when they are kneeling the saddles are high from the ground, and we have to mount them by ladders.

Then the drivers straddle the necks of the elephants, each putting his legs just behind the great flapping ears.

We are told to hold tight to the framework of the saddle, and then the drivers prod the beasts with their steel hooks, and give them the signal to rise. The great elephants grunt as they slowly raise us upward, and we go off in a swinging walk through the city.

We are as high up in the air as though we were on the roof of a village house, and the servants who run along on the road below us seem very far down. The motion is a swaying one, and at first it has the effect of a rolling ship, making us almost seasick. After a time we become used to it, and soon begin to enjoy our strange ride. We go out of the city and climb up the sides of the mountains near by.

The road passes through some of the wild country scenes of native India. The people are very kind to wild animals, and all things having life are respected by them. Nothing we meet seems to fear us. We pass through woods in which monkeys jump from tree to tree, and now and then one of them hops across the road in front of the elephants, frightening the beasts so that they jump backward and almost throw us to the ground. We see wild peacocks spreading their gorgeous tails out under the rays of the sun, and along the slopes of the mountains we meet wild hogs. At times we pass between hedges of cactuses twelve feet in height, and not far from Jaipur we skirt a lake, on the banks of which we see half a dozen great black crocodiles sleeping in the sun.

The tame animals we pass on the road are quite as curious as the wild ones that we see in the woods. We go by droves of little donkeys so loaded down with great bags and baskets that only their legs show out, and the loads seem to be walking off by themselves. The donkeys are no bigger than Newfoundland dogs, and their dark-skinned drivers, barelegged, pound and yell at them in Hindustani, as they drive them along without either bridle or rein.

Here comes a stage pulled by a camel. It is filled with black-faced passengers who are on their way to Jaipur to trade. We pass other camels ridden by men, women, and boys, who look at us with inquiring eyes as we ride by on our elephants.

Some of the camel riders are by no means polite, as you may see from the shabby trick which one of them played upon me when I was once before riding upon one of these very elephants of the Rajah of Jaipur. We were several miles from the city, and my elephant was rolling along at a good round pace. The flies swarmed about us by thousands, and half covered the elephant. They persisted in attacking my eyes and face. I had to hold on tight to the elephant saddle with one hand, and my other hand was busy in carrying the umbrella which kept off the rays of the tropical sun.

Just then a long-legged, black-skinned Hindu came up on a camel. He was tormented by so many flies that they covered his white gown and made the skin of his camel appear almost black. As he drew near my elephant he took his whip and gave his camel a cut. The beast came toward us on the trot. Just as he reached us the Hindu unwound the shawl which formed his long white turban, and with this swept both sides of his camel as he passed by. The flies left him and attacked me and the elephant, and I could hear his laugh ringing out on the air as he trotted ahead.

After a time we reach the famous old ruined city of Ambir, and then ride back to Jaipur. At the hotel our elephants kneel, and we crawl down the ladder, thoroughly tired out by the journey.

In the Himalayas.

XXX. ABOVE THE CLOUDS; OR, NATURE AND MAN IN THE HEART OF THE HIMALAYA MOUNTAINS.

LET us now leave the lowlands of India, and take a trip among the snowy peaks of the Himalaya Mountains. They are the highest mountains of the globe. The word *Himalaya* means "the abode of snow," and these mountains are crowned with eternal frost. The tops of many of them have never been reached by man. Mount Everest, in the Himalayas, is the highest mountain of the world. It is 29,002 feet in height, or more than twice as high as Fusiyama, the sacred snow-capped mountain of Japan. Mont Blanc, the tallest of the Alps, is less than sixteen thousand feet high. If you went to the top of Mont Blanc, and from there in a balloon ascended straight upward, you would have to rise a distance of more than two miles before you would reach the altitude of Mount Everest.

The Himalaya Mountains extend in the shape of a double wall, with a wide, irregular trough or valley between them, along the northern boundary of Hindustan. If you could stretch the Himalaya range over the United States, beginning at New York, it would reach almost to Denver. Its average width would be nearly as great as the distance between New York and Washington, and the mountains of the southern wall, corresponding to those nearest India, would rise steeply up from the plains to a height of almost twenty thousand feet, or nearly four miles.

The Himalayas have scores of peaks, each of which is higher than Mont Blanc, and at least forty of which rise more than one mile higher than that famous monarch of the Alps. It is said that you could drop all of the Alps into some of the valleys of the Himalayas, and at a distance of ten miles from them there would be no perceptible change in the face of nature.

We read much about the glaciers, or moving masses of ice and snow, in the mountains of Switzerland. In the Himalayas there are moving fields of solid ice from thirty to sixty miles in length, and one of them, thirty-three miles long, lies between two mountains, each of which is more than five miles in height.

The scenery upon these mountains is unlike that of the Rockies or the Alps. The Himalayas lie on the edge of the tropics, and the moisture rising from the Indian plains gives them a thousand clouds where the Alps have one.

As we travel up them, or climb about their rocky recesses, we see great masses of vapor of all kinds and shapes chasing each other over the hills below us. At the distance of two miles above the sea the clouds crawl up the steep sides of the valleys and climb to our very feet. Soon they wrap themselves around us, and for a few moments the mist is so thick that we cannot see the heads of the horses upon which we are riding. A moment later the clouds have passed. They float onward and lose themselves among the snows above.

During our travels in the Himalayas we shall often have clouds above and below us. In the hollows in the sides of the mountains we shall see queer-shaped clouds, which at times look almost like men who have sat down for a rest. At other times the clouds appear to have taken the forms of beasts, and in single file race through the air. In the morning the sun gilds the clouds so that they become masses of fire, and at night the moon turns them to curious creatures of silver and gold. In the early morning the valleys of the Himalayas are filled with mists, and as we gaze down upon them from the mountains we seem to be standing above an icy ocean. As we look we may see the sun rise. It kisses the tops of the highest peaks, and makes the snow upon them shine with all the colors of the rainbow.

We shall visit these wonderful mountains at Darjiling, a little village lying under the shadows of a number of the highest Himalaya peaks. It is situated in the hills about a mile and a half above the level of the sea. The climate there is cold, although it is not very far north of Calcutta, from which we make our start to-day. The plains of India are in the tropics. We ride over them on the railroad, and at last, near the foothills, we dash into jungles containing great thickets of bamboo and hundreds of banyan trees, which send scores of sprouts down from their branches into the earth, and make the jungle almost impenetrable. There are thousands of curious plants, there are poisonous vines, and great trees so thick that we can see only a few steps from the train through the green.

"Our motive power"

The jungles are the home of the tiger, and as we go through them we may see the bright eyes of this beast staring out of the darkness.

At the foot of the mountains we take the little narrow-gauge railroad that carries us up to Darjiling. It is only two feet wide, and it curves in and out among the trees like a great snake. Our motive power is a little steam engine which carries us upward more than a thousand feet every hour. There are a dozen horseshoe curves every mile. There are numerous loops, and we cross our track again and again in making the gradual slope which will permit of our being carried further up into the clouds. At times we pass precipices covered with green, down which, out of the car windows, we can look for a thousand feet; and then we climb along the sides of the mountains above valleys which fade away into the broad plains of Bengal.

We soon leave the jungle and find in its place huge forest trees, some of which are two hundred feet high. The trees are clothed with a luxuriant growth of moss and ferns; and we see orchids, curious flowers of many beautiful colors and shapes, fastened to their trunks and hanging from their branches. As we rise still further we notice the tree fern. This has a tall, round trunk from ten to twenty feet in length, from the top of which immense fern leaves jut out like the leaves of a palm.

The air is full of moisture, and the vegetation, though not so thick as in the jungle, is still luxuriant. As we rise still higher, the color of the moss on the trees changes from a brilliant green to frosted silver. It is now somewhat like the Spanish moss which is to be found in some of our Southern States. This moss clings to the limbs of the trees like a coat. It hangs from their branches in clusters, and makes them look in the distance like a forest of green dusted with silver.

At about a mile above the plains we find many of the trees of our American mountains. Roses are blooming in the villages, and the sides of some of the hills are covered with immense tea gardens, much like those we saw in Japan.

Tea Plant.

The tea plant grows wild in some parts of the Himalayas. Its natural home is said to be Assam, one of the northeastern provinces of India, where travelers say it sometimes reaches the size of a large tree. It is supposed that the plant was originally taken from this side of the Himalayas, and introduced into China, from where it was carried to Japan.

By far the greater part of the tea of commerce was produced in China and Japan until within a few years. The British, however, have now planted tea gardens in India,

"We see groups of natives, known as Leptchas"

and they are raising delicious tea. That produced in the Himalayas is shipped to all parts of the world. The plant is grown also in the island of Ceylon, and the people of the United States now use hundreds of thousands of pounds of Indian tea.

We pass a number of villages on our journey up the mountains. The cars are surrounded at each stop by curious people. We see groups of natives, known as

Leptchas, who have faces not unlike those of our American Indians. The men are short, with broad chests, big calves, and long arms. They have copper-colored faces and thick, coal-black hair, which they wear in long plaits down their backs. The women have two braids of hair, and both sexes wear robes of striped, coarse cotton cloth which fall to below their knees, leaving their arms free.

During the rainy season they all wear high boots of deerskin, as a protection from the terrible leeches which are then found in the mountains. These leeches are so numerous that in a half hour's walk over the grass more than one hundred of them may be found to have fastened themselves upon you. They suck your blood, and they have been known to live for days in the jaws, nostrils, and stomachs of human beings, causing dreadful suffering and death.

The Leptcha women load themselves with jewelry, and, like the women of the other hill tribes of the Himalaya Mountains, are fond of ornaments of all kinds. We see many girls who have bracelets of silver covering their arms from their wrists to their elbows, and some who have heavy rings of gold and silver about their ankles. Some have flat pieces of gold hanging from their ears, and not a few have jeweled buttons fastened in the flesh of their noses.

The Bhutanese are another hill tribe which we find in the Himalaya Mountains. They look not unlike the Leptchas, and they dress much the same, except that they paint their faces with a sort of brown varnish. Nearly every Bhutanese woman wears the greater part of her fortune. Some have large beads of coral and turquoise bound about their heads. Some have earrings of gold so heavy that they pull down the lobes of their ears; and the poorest are covered with jewelry of brass or stone, if they cannot afford silver and gold.

The women of the Himalaya Mountains are very strong. We see them digging in the fields. They act as porters, carrying great quantities of grain and other things in baskets fastened to their backs. Sometimes even babies are so carried.

When we arrive at the station of Darjiling we are met by rosy-cheeked girls who offer to carry our trunks and other baggage up to the hotel. We hesitate a moment at the idea of allowing women to do such things for us, but finally consent, and each of these lusty girls picks up a trunk weighing perhaps two hundred pounds, swings it upon her back, and trots off with it up the hill. The charge is an amount equal to about five cents of our money.

The men of the Himalaya Mountains are fully as strong as the women. Each one of them carries a great knife in his belt, and many of them are very fierce-looking.

The mountaineers live in low huts not much larger than dry-goods boxes. They are made of mud and stone, and have roofs of straw thatch. The people do most of their cooking out of doors. They eat with their fingers. They sleep on the floor, and have but little civilization. They are worshipers of Buddha, and are much like the people of Tibet, whom we shall visit in the next chapter.

"even babies are so carried."

XXXI. TIBET AND THE TIBETANS.

THE Tibetans do not allow foreigners to come into their country, and those who do so run the risk of losing their lives. A famous Hindu, Baboo Chandra Das, in 1890 traveled through Tibet, spending some time in Lassa, the capital of the country. He had to disguise himself as a Tibetan in order to make the journey. In 1846, a Catholic priest named Huc was able to make his way through Tibet and to spend some time in Lassa by dressing up as a Tibetan. We have our latest knowledge of the northern part of the country from an American explorer, W. W. Rockhill, who entered Tibet by way of Mongolia in 1892.

A Tibetan Chief.

The Hindus call Tibet the Roof of the World. The country consists of an immense table-land, about one fifth the size of the United States. It lies between two ranges of mountains, and the greater part of it is more than two miles above the sea. This plateau of Tibet has a number of large rivers, and it contains both fresh- and salt-water lakes. Its largest stream is the Yaru Tsangbu, or Yaru River, which flows for seven hundred miles through southern Tibet, and is supposed to empty finally into the Brahmaputra River. The Indus rises in the western part of Tibet, and the

Yangtze and the Hoang, the two great rivers of China, have their sources in the northeastern part of the country. Tibet is a very rough land, and is cut up by several mountain chains. It has many desert plains, and northeast of it lies the great Desert of Gobi.

The climate of Tibet is exceedingly dry. In the summer, which lasts from May to October, the valleys are hot, though the mountains are covered with snow. In the winter the leaves of the trees wither and become so dry that they may be ground to powder between the fingers. Planks and beams crack and break from the extreme dryness of the air, and the Tibetans sometimes cover the woodwork of their houses with coarse cotton to preserve them.

There is no danger from dampness. The Tibetans need neither refrigerators nor salt to keep their food. Meat of all kinds can be left out of doors without spoiling. The dry air sucks up the juices, and the flesh soon becomes so dry that it can be powdered like bread. When once powdered it can be kept for years, and mutton cured in this way is a common food in Tibet. As soon as a sheep is killed it is skinned, cleaned, and hung up out of doors. It quickly becomes a dry, stiffened mass, and is often kept for a long time.

As is common among the people of cold climates, the Tibetans are very fond of fats, and one of their favorite dishes is a soup made of brick tea mixed with salt, butter, and water, and cooked into a thick, fatty broth. After the broth is taken off the fire, it is thickened with barley meal, the mixture being churned together in a little tea churn. When served it is ladled out into bowls, and the people knead the mush into dough pellets with their fingers before eating it.

Both women and men are fond of tobacco, and they use it largely in the shape of snuff, carrying it in horn boxes which look much like our powderhorns.

It is estimated that there are about three million Tibetans living upon this dry, cold Asiatic plateau. They are divided into many different tribes, each of which has curious customs.

Many of the Tibetans look much like our American Indians. They have high cheek bones, and those who are exposed to the sun have copper-colored complexions. None of the men have beards, and all carry pincers to pluck the hairs out of their faces. Mr. Rockhill found some tribes of Tibetans who had curly hair, and others whose hair was as straight as that of our Indians.

Tibetan Coat.

The different tribes dress much alike, wearing in the winter sheepskin gowns with the wool turned inward, or so many other furs that it is often hard to tell where the clothes end and the people begin. In summer the gowns are made of native woolen cloth. The dresses of both sexes reach from the neck to below the knees, and are tied about the waist with woolen girdles. The people are fond of bright colors, and have clothes of red, purple, and yellow. Both men and women have very large boots, which are sometimes made of red or yellow leather, and are held up by bright-colored garters.

In some parts of the country the men shave their heads, and in these sections hats are always worn. In northern Tibet both men and women wear caps of green, red, or blue

"Both men and women have very large boots—"

cloth, which are sometimes faced with lambskin. In the winter time the men wear pointed caps of felt, which are often covered with blue or red silk, and which have large ear flaps.

"—the hats are high—"

Some of the Tibetan men never trim their hair except to cut it in front so that it makes a fringe just over the eyes. Behind, it hangs down to their shoulders and forms a sufficient protection against the weather. In some places the hats are high and shaped much like those of Korean gentlemen, with fully as broad brims, and with much bigger crowns. These hats are very gorgeous indeed. Their brims are often faced with red or blue cotton or silk, the hat being held on by a string around the throat.

Both men and women are fond of jewelry, the men frequently wearing an earring in the left ear. Such earrings are sometimes set with pearls and turquoises, and are often two inches long. The women wear chains of gold, silver, and copper about their necks. They wear earrings, some of which are so heavy that a little strap is tied to them and passed over the top of the ear to take the weight from the lobe. They adorn their hair with many kinds of jeweled trinkets, plaiting gold, silver, amber, and coral ornaments in with their braids.

Some of the Tibetans live in tents made of the hair of the yak or mountain cow, and others have rude houses of wood or stone. The houses of the rich are sometimes of three stories. They are built around a simple court, and often contain a number of rooms. The houses of the poor are generally of two stories, with a courtyard in front or behind, and with the ground floor used as a stable.

The walls of the houses are usually put together without cement. The windows are little holes which are closed at night with wooden shutters. The roofs are flat, those of the larger rooms being supported by wooden pillars. They are covered with earth in most parts of the country, and are often used as threshing floors. The ground floors are generally of earth, but those of the better class are paved with stone or pebbles set in clay and well pounded down.

The Tibetan houses have but little furniture. The people sit on the floor, and they sleep upon mats or skins. They light their houses with lamps filled with butter in which a little cotton wick is stuck; and where butter is scarce they sometimes use chips of pitch pine which they burn on a flat stone in the middle of the room. As a rule, however, the Tibetans go to sleep as soon as it becomes dark, and use no other light than that of the sun. Some of the houses have cooking stoves of clay which are heated by little fires made of dry manure.

There are not many large cities in Tibet, and it is only here and there that the villages are of any size. Lassa, the capital, is said to contain about fifty thousand people, and it has the finest buildings of the country. These are monasteries. The Tibetans are Buddhists. The country is ruled by Buddhist priests, or lamas, of whom there are about one hundred thousand in Tibet.

At the head of the lamas is the Grand Lama, who lives in a temple just outside of Lassa, and who is usually a boy. When Chandra Das, the Hindu explorer, visited Lassa, the grand lama was only eight years old. Chandra Das says that the grand lama's temple is on a mountain, and that it has many golden domes, and is wonderfully beautiful. He had to climb up ladders to reach the temple, and he got down on his knees before this little boy priest whom all the Tibetans worship.

The Tibetans are very religious. They are always praying, and they have machines of different kinds with which they pray to Buddha. These are called prayer wheels. A number of prayers are written out upon a strip of paper. The paper is wrapped around a stick and inclosed in a little tin or brass box so that by swinging the stick the paper turns around within the box; and the man believes that at every turn he gets the credit of as many prayers as are written upon it. Sometimes prayer wheels are turned by the wind, and in some places you see them so arranged that the wheel is made to go around by the water of some creek or brook. When a man wants to pray he pulls out a peg, and the wind or water prays for him, wiping out a sin, so he thinks, with each turn of the wheel. Nearly all education in Tibet is confined to the priesthood, and Tibetan books are almost altogether religious.

One of the queerest of Tibetan customs is in regard to marriage. Instead of one man having several wives, as is

Tibetans

common in most Asiatic countries, here one woman has several husbands. When a Tibetan girl marries into a family, she often becomes the wife of all the brothers of her husband. She is the head of the domestic affairs of the household, and she is expected to take care of the home, do the cooking, and work in the fields. In the towns nearly all the shops are kept by women, and the Tibetan wife's opinion is usually asked by her husband. She does not think that she has a hard time, and a rich Tibetan lady whom Chandra Das met in Lassa told him that she pitied the women of other countries, who were so poor that they could have only one husband.

The Tibetans have mines of gold, silver, and copper. Beautiful turquoise is found in some parts of the country, and is brought to India for sale. The people raise small quantities of wheat, barley, and potatoes, and they have some fruits, such as peaches, grapes, and apples.

The Tibetans are stock breeders, however, rather than farmers. Many of them have large flocks of sheep and goats, and some have herds of yaks or mountain cows. The yak is used for carrying burdens up the hills, being very sure-footed and strong. A yak is about as large as a good-sized cow. Its body is covered with a thick coat of black and white hair about two inches long. It has horns like those of a cow, and its tail, which is like that of a horse, though much more bushy, is in many cases three feet in length. The yak has a hump upon its shoulders which is largely composed of fat, and its hoofs are like those of our cattle.

Another beast that is found in Tibet is the musk deer, from which comes a large part of the musk perfume of commerce. This animal is smaller than the deer which we have in America. The musk is found in the form of fat in a little sac beneath the skin of the abdomen. The sack is about as large as a small orange, and its contents, which are of a dark brown or chocolate color, look much like moist gingerbread. When the animal is killed, the ball of musk fat is taken out and dried. It is then shipped over the mountains to India and China, and from there it is exported to this country and to Europe, where it forms the basis of many perfumes.

XXXII. PERSIA AND THE PERSIANS.

TRAVELING westward across northwestern India, we ride on horses and camels through wild mountain passes and over high plains, on our way to Persia, and finally come to the vast Plateau of Irän', which includes Afghanistän', Baluchistän', and Persia, the three countries comprising a territory about one third the size of the United States. Afghanistan and Baluchistan are occupied by nomads, or wandering tribes, who own large flocks of sheep, goats, and yaks. They have few manufactures, and raise practically nothing for export.

The Plateau of Iran.

The men are straight-eyed and dark-faced. They wear turbans and gowns, and nearly every one we meet carries a gun or a sword.

The people of these two nations are almost altogether Mohammedans. Afghanistan is ruled by the ameer, who lives in the city of Kabul. This city is situated about a mile above the sea, and contains about seventy-five thousand people. Baluchistan has a ruler called the khan, who lives at Khelat, a city with fourteen thousand inhabitants.

Commerce is carried on entirely by caravan. There are

266   PERSIA.

A Nomad Family and House.

few roads and no railroads, and though both countries contain fertile valleys, they are for the most part made up of vast tracts of mountainous lands and deserts occupied by wild animals. We may see herds of wild asses, and if we should pass through the forests we might be in danger from lions, tigers, leopards, and wolves.

The country of Persia looks very small upon the map, but it is really larger than France, Germany, Great Britain and Ireland put together. It consists of a high table-land lying about three quarters of a mile above the sea, with a rim of mountains around it. The slopes that run down to the Caspian Sea are covered with timber, but the hills that slope inward, and the table-land itself, are made up largely of barren deserts, some of which are covered with salt, while others contain great quantities of sulphur. One salt desert in Persia is about as large as the States of

New York and Pennsylvania. A great part of the land cannot be cultivated, and only about one fourth of it is now farmed. The Persians have thousands of little irrigating canals, and many of their fields are watered from wells.

Persia produces excellent wheat, barley, millet, and maize. It has much cotton, tobacco, and opium. Its fruits are delicious, and among them are grapes, peaches, oranges, dates, and lemons. Dates are sold very cheap, some kinds bringing only about one half cent a pound.

Street Scene in Tabriz, Persia.

There are no railroads in Persia. We must make our way through it on camel or mule paths, and we shall have to travel in caravans in order to be safe. We find that most of the people live in villages, that they may the better defend themselves from robbers and wandering tribes. The villages are usually surrounded by high walls. Their gates are closed at night, and the flocks and herds are driven in before dark and kept inside until morning.

The houses are made of mud, and they are seldom of more than one story. They have flat roofs, and look more like great square or oblong mud boxes than houses. They are built along narrow, unpaved streets which are full of dust and dirt. Nearly every house has a stable beside it, and the yard of the stable is the same as that of the house. In some of the yards we find the women molding manure into cakes, such as we saw in India, and sticking them on the walls to dry. There are few trees, except on the mountains, and such cakes are the fuel of a large part of Persia.

Outside of each village there are threshing floors. These are places about twenty-five feet square, where the ground has been rolled until it is as hard as stone. The wheat or barley is cut with sickles and brought from the fields on donkeys to the threshing floors, where oxen are driven around over it until every grain is trodden out. Then with wooden pitchforks the farmers toss up the straw until the chaff is all blown aside. They keep the straw for feeding the sheep, donkeys, and oxen.

Donkeys and camels are, to a large extent, the beasts of burden in Persia. We see droves of donkeys everywhere carrying heavy loads, and on the long desert journeys everything goes upon camels.

The Persian sheep produce excellent wool. The most curious thing about them is their tails, which are very fat; a single tail often weighs as much as ten pounds. Mr. S. G. Wilson, a missionary who lived a long time in Persia, says that the Persians often milk their sheep and goats, and he describes an odd custom which they have in order to make the cows give down their milk. They think that a cow will become dry if it knows that its calf has been

Cooking Chops in the Streets of Tcheran, Persia.

taken away, so they try to deceive the cow. After killing the calf, they take its hide and stuff it with straw, and place this stuffed calf beside the cow at milking time.

But let us take a look at the people of Persia. There are about nine millions of them, and the most of them have cream-colored faces, straight eyes, and dark hair. The men shave their heads and wear long cloths wrapped around

"—where oxen are driven around over it

them in the shape of a turban. Many wear high, cone-shaped hats of rough felt. The women cover their heads with red handkerchiefs, and when they go out upon the streets they always wear veils.

Both sexes of the poorer Persians wear cotton gowns, those of the men falling to their feet, and those of the women reaching only to the knees, leaving their limbs and feet bare. The women of the well-to-do class have a street costume consisting partly of very full trousers gathered in about the ankles and tied above their fine leather shoes, which are turned up at the toes. Over their shoulders they wear a piece of fine cloth about two yards square, which is put on over the head and covers up the whole person. Such costumes are of blue, black, or striped goods, the women all wearing about the same colors, so that it is hard for a man to tell his own wife if he meets her on the streets. The house dress is different. Indoors the women wear divided skirts which reach to the knees, and loose-fitting sacks with very long sleeves.

Persian women have to keep in their own part of the house. It would be a disgrace for them to be seen by other men than those of their own family; and before a caller enters the gate, he is expected to shout out some such words as "Woman, away!" in order to give the women a chance to fly into their own quarters.

When a Persian lady of high rank takes a walk through the streets, she often has an attendant with her who goes before her and orders all men to turn their eyes in another direction. A Persian never asks after the wives of his friends, and if a caller should be so impolite as to do so, the host in his reply would not speak of his wife by name, or as his wife, but would refer to her as his children's mother. For instance, suppose that the Persian's name is Smith, and that he has a son named John. Upon being asked as to his wife, he will not reply "My wife is well," or "Mrs. Smith is well," but may say, "I thank you, little Johnnie's mother is so-so to-day."

The Persian women, in fact, have very few rights, and they are mostly slaves of their husbands. Parents arrange most of the marriages. Girls are often betrothed when they are young, and are sometimes married under ten.

A Group of Persian Women.

The Persians have ideas of beauty different from ours. Their women to be beautiful must be fat, and a face as round as the moon is much desired. They are proud of high foreheads and heavy eyebrows, and they sometimes paint their brows to make them look thicker than they are.

The poorer women do all kinds of housework. They milk the cows, prepare the fuel, and do all the cooking. They do not have much trouble in taking care of the furniture. The floor of most Persian houses forms the beds, the tables, and the chairs of the family. The people lie upon mattresses at night, using no sheets, and covering themselves with a very thick quilt. In the daytime the bedding is rolled up and put away in a corner.

All eating is done with the fingers, and the plates of the poorer families are often thin cakes of bread. A man usually eats his plate after he is through with his dinner, and during the meal he tears off a piece of it, and by bending it up picks out bits of meat from the soup and conveys them to his mouth. The diet of the common people is largely made up of bread, cheese, and milk, with a little meat in the form of a stew, or soup, once a day. The Persians drink a great deal of tea, and are fond of coffee.

Persia has not many large cities. Tĕ-heran' contains about two hundred thousand people, and is the place where the shah, the despotic ruler of the country, lives. There is a wall and a deep moat around Teheran. The city has many fine buildings, and among other institutions a college where about two hundred and fifty Persian and Armenian boys are educated after modern methods.

The great business city of Persia is Tabriz', situated on a plain in the northern part of the country. It is about as large as Teheran, but it has not so many fine buildings. It is, in fact, made up of a vast number of one- and two-story houses with mud walls surrounding them. These are close to the streets, and the streets are so narrow that in going through them we have to crowd against the walls to keep out of the way of the donkeys and camels. The walls are from ten to twenty-five feet high, and keep the men from looking in and seeing the women.

The business of the Persian cities is done almost alto-

In a Persian Bazaar.

gether in bazaars, much like those we saw in India. The merchants sit in their little shops in turbans and gowns, as they work and sell. There are, it is estimated, about five thousand such shops in Tabriz, the most of which are not more than ten feet square. Each merchant has his goods piled around him, and you bargain for hours before you make many purchases, because the Persian always asks several times as much as he expects to get, and will not lower the price without much talk.

In our travels through Persia we shall find that the people are not very civilized. The officers can be bribed, and the most terrible punishments are inflicted. For very small offenses men are often whipped on their bare feet with canes. A man is placed on the ground, and his feet are fastened into a board which is raised so that his soles slant upward and can be easily beaten. The right hands of thieves are sometimes cut off. A few years ago a famous robber chief was caught and put alive into the mouth of a loaded cannon. The cannon was then fired, and the man was blown into pieces.

There is not much education in Persia, and little more than reading, writing, and arithmetic is anywhere taught. The boys go to school in the mosques or temples. The master reads the lessons, and the children repeat them after him. There are no schools for girls, and very few of the women of Persia know how to read.

XXXIII. ARABIA, OR LIFE IN THE DESERT.

OUR best way to go to Arabia will be to return to India and take one of the steamships that sail weekly from Bombay to A'den. Aden is the chief seaport of Arabia. The ships going from Europe to India, Australia, and China by way of the Suez Canal take on coal at Aden, and the great steamers which carry tea and other things from Asia to Europe also stop at this port. The different tribes of southern Arabia come to Aden to trade, and from Aden are shipped much of the famed Mocha coffee, ostrich feathers, fruit, and other things raised by the Arabs.

Aden.

It takes us a week to sail from Bombay to Aden. Our first sight of land gives us a fair idea of many parts of the Arabian peninsula. There is no country which is less inviting and more desolate. Imagine a great harbor of sea-green water, the shores of which rise almost straight upward in the shape of a ragged mountain of brown rock and white sand. There is not a tree or a blade of grass to be seen. All is gray, brown, and dazzling white.

The city of Aden itself does not relieve the picture. Its houses are white and brown, being mostly one- and two-story buildings made of sun-dried brick and covered with plaster. Along the edges of the hills there are huts of the same brown color as the rocks themselves. Everything is dusty and dirty, and as soon as we land, the hot, dry air of the desert almost parches our tongues, and we ask for a drink.

We find that water is worth money in Aden, and that every one pays for all that he gets. It rains very seldom, and often two years pass without a drop falling. There is only one well in the city. The most of the water used is made by machines which evaporate sea water, leaving the salt behind, and condense the steam into fresh water. Aden is under the control of the British, and these machines belong to the British government, which sells the water to the people, and gives a certain amount every day to each of the British soldiers who are stationed there.

Arabia is one of the least-known countries of the world. It is about one third the size of the whole United States, and a line drawn diagonally across it from the Isthmus of Suez to the town of Maskat, on the Arabian Sea, would be longer than the distance between Boston and New Orleans.

Arabia and Turkey in Asia.

This vast territory has no railroads, no great rivers, and very little soil that is good for farming. Most of the southern part of Arabia, on the edge of which is Aden, has never been explored by Europeans or Americans. It is known, however, that Arabia is largely made up of rocky deserts like that about Aden, and that a great part of it is a vast plateau more than half a mile above the sea.

Arabia contains a population about as large as that of the State of New York. We find the people very fine-looking. The men are straight and well formed. They have dark faces, coarse black hair, and aquiline noses. Here comes one of them leading his camel. He wears a long white cotton gown or shirt which is open at the chest, and which is bound around his waist with a girdle of leather. He has a goat's-hair cloak of black and white stripes thrown over his shoulders, and his head is covered with a bright yellow silk handkerchief which is tied on with a black band of twisted hair about as big around as your finger. This band is bound around his head, and the long end of the handkerchief hangs down upon his shoulders. His ankles and feet are bare, though his feet are protected from the hot streets by sandals.

Arab Girl.

Behind him comes a woman. She wears a gown which is open at the neck and which falls to her feet. A piece of dark blue cloth covers her head and the most of her figure, and trails on the ground behind her. She does not wear the veil which is common in Persia, nor does she conceal her face so carefully as the women whom we saw in India.

The inhabitants of Arabia may be divided into two great classes — those who live in tents, and those who dwell in the towns and villages. The tent dwellers are generally known as Bed'ou-ins. They are the wandering tribes who pick out the good pasture grounds, and upon them graze

"The tent dwellers—"

the flocks of sheep and the herds of camels from which they get their living. They are the people of the desert, and we shall meet more of them as we go northward through Syria. They are a very bold race, and are hostile to strangers. If we should attempt to pass through Arabia we should have to go upon camels, and in order to travel with any safety we must pay a tribute to the Bedouin chiefs, or sheiks, to keep them from robbing us.

The Bedouin tents are generally made of cloth of goat's hair dyed black. A tent is seldom more than twenty feet long, but it usually has one part shut off for the women and children. There is no furniture to speak of. The cooking is done over an open fire, and all the family eat with their fingers. The Bedouins wear but little clothing. The boys go naked until they are thirteen, and the girls until they are seven.

Some of the tent dwellers raise a little wheat and barley, but millet is their chief crop. Millet and dates form the principal food of the Arabs. The millet is ground to flour and made into cakes. The date comes from the date palm, and it is eaten by the horses and camels as well as by the people.

We have all heard of the wonderful Arabian horses, but in Arabia camels are much more important animals than horses. They carry almost all the burdens, and it is upon them that the Bedouins travel when they move from one place to another.

There are riding camels and freight camels. The riding camels are the more gentle. Some of them are very rapid travelers, making six miles an hour and keeping up this pace for fifteen hours every day for a week at a time. They are very valuable in passing through the deserts, because they can go a long distance without food or water. A camel can store away enough water at one drinking to last him for a week.

The best Arabian horses are produced in the province of Nejd, in central Arabia. They are not so large as the average American horse, and we have many race horses which can go faster than they can. They are usually gray in color, though some of them are chestnut, sorrel, or black. They are noted for their beauty, for their kind-

An Arab and His Horse.

ness, and for their endurance. They are trained to travel long distances without water, and a good Arabian horse can canter for twenty-four hours in summer, and for forty-eight in winter, without drinking.

The Bedouins think a great deal of their horses. These animals are brought up by their masters almost as carefully as though they were children, and they are seldom sold. The Bedouins ride them with halters instead of bridles, guiding them this way and that with the knee.

The Arabian villages look more like dust heaps than anything else. They are surrounded by mud walls. The houses are seldom of more than two stories, and the majority are of only one story. They have flat roofs, and are made of bricks dried in the sun. Each village is cut up by winding, narrow streets, and such shops as it has are built about a market place where the people come to trade. The shops are often kept by women, and very little else than food is sold in them.

But suppose we make a visit to one of the high-class Arabs. His house is like all Arabian town houses, only a little better than that of the average native. We pass through a low door, and into a large coffee or reception room. Here all guests are received, and if we should stay over night it is here that we should sleep, on the floor.

Our host is a well-to-do man, and we find the room covered with carpets. There are cushions here and there, and we take seats on the floor. At one end of the room there is a fireplace. Upon this some coffee is steaming, and we are offered a cup as soon as we are seated. It is served in little china cups, as big around as an eggshell. The fluid is as thick as molasses and as hot as fire. We sip it gingerly, and enjoy the rich aromatic smell.

We find our Arabian friends very hospitable, so we

stay until evening, and are then asked to take dinner. Many of the Arabs eat only one full meal a day, this being served soon after sunset. Our dinner consists of thin wheat cakes baked to a crisp on an oven, and of a stew of tough camel's flesh.

We eat with our fingers, and pick the meat out of the stew with pieces of the wheat cakes, which we double up for the purpose. Then dates and other fruits and sweets are offered to us. When we have finished, a bowl of water is brought in and every one washes his hands. Then a covered bowl with incense burning in it is passed around to each guest, in order that he may perfume his hands, face, and clothes. No liquor is served. Very few Arabs drink wine; for they are Mohammedans, and the drinking of intoxicating liquors is against the rules of their religion.

We find the people very simple in their habits and very clean as to their persons. They bathe often, and are especially careful of their teeth, which shine out like rows of ivory from the dark backgrounds of their complexions. Nearly all the men and boys shave their heads, as is the custom with all good Mohammedans, and not a few of the men in the cities wear large white turbans.

We find that the Arabs have very bright minds, though they are almost altogether uneducated, and very few can read. A thousand years ago the Arabs were among the most learned people of the world. They had the best doctors, and they were also famous as mathematicians and astronomers. They were the first to introduce the study of algebra into western Europe, and they were early noted for their knowledge of geography.

Arabia was long the seat of the Mohammedan religion, and the city of Mecca, where Mohammed was born, is still a holy place to the millions of people who believe in this religion. Mecca has about forty-five thousand inhabitants. It lies in a sandy valley surrounded by rocky hills in the interior of the country, seventy-five miles east of the Red Sea. Pilgrims by the thousand come on camels in caravans from Turkey south through Palestine to Mecca, and many go by ship to Jiddah, which is the seaport for Mecca, and from there travel inland on camels, or on foot.

Mecca contains a great mosque or Mohammedan temple covering more than an acre, in which is a famous black stone. This stone, according to the native tradition, fell out of paradise when Adam was thrust out of the Garden of Eden. The Mohammedans believe that if they kiss it their sins will pass away as their lips touch the rock. This stone is now black. According to tradition, it was originally whiter than snow, but the Mo-

A Mohammedan at Prayer.

hammedans say, that, having been kissed through many generations, the sins of the people have gone into it and turned it black. The real nature of the stone shows that it is of meteoric origin, and we know that there are many similar stones in other parts of the world.

XXXIV. PALESTINE AND ITS PEOPLE.

LEAVING Aden, we prepare for a tour through the great Turkish Empire (map on p. 275). Turkey in Asia comprises the western and northeastern parts of Arabia, and takes in Palestine and the whole of Asia Minor. We may begin our trip by sailing around the southern coast of Arabia, through the Persian Gulf, and up the river Euphrates, or we may take one of a regular line of steamers and go through the long Red Sea and the Suez Canal into the Mediterranean. The first route would be through the pearl fisheries of the Persian Gulf, and we should see native divers by hundreds gathering pearls.

The Arabs are expert divers. We see something of them in the harbor of Aden. Little black fellows wearing nothing but a cloth tied around their waists swim about like turtles in the water near our steamer, waiting for us to throw coins into the ocean in order that they may dive down and catch them before they fall to the bottom. They do not speak our language, but they have picked up a few words, which they shout at us something like this:

"Hab-a-dive? Hab-a-dive? Hab-a-dive?"

They sing out the words, showing their white teeth as they do so. Some are in canoes. There are perhaps a hundred about the ship, swimming and rowing. We throw out a silver coin, the size of a ten-cent piece. As it strikes the water a score of black boys dive for it. A moment later one comes up and turns his face toward us, and we see the coin shining out between his white teeth.

The best pearl beds of the world are those opposite Bahrein in the Persian Gulf, where from one to two million dollars' worth of pearls are found every year. There are

Jerusalem from the Mount of Olives.

many villages of Arabs here which are supported by the pearl fisheries. The divers wear only a girdle about the waist, to which a basket is fastened. They plug up their ears and noses, and tie great stones to their feet in order that they may the more easily remain under the water.

Pearls, you know, come from oysters, the beds of which are away down at the bottom of the sea. The divers gather the oysters and fill their baskets, and then, giving a signal, they are drawn up by means of cords which are fastened to their bodies.

The oysters yield the best pearls when they are about four years old, and pearls, we find, are of value according to their shape and the beauty of their tint. Those which are perfectly round are the most prized, and the finest pearl known to the world is in a museum at Moscow, Russia. The largest known pearl is in the South Kensington Museum in England; it weighs three ounces. It is as big round as a walnut, but its shape is not a perfect sphere. The pearls found in Arabia are of all sizes, some being no larger than a mustard seed.

The route to Asia Minor passes along the Euphrates and the Tigris up to the old city of Bagdad, and thence by caravan over the country to Aleppo. But we wish first to visit Palestine, so we take the other route. Sailing over the Red Sea for fourteen hundred miles, we float through the Suez Canal and into the Mediterranean. We land at Jaffa (the ancient Joppa), a ragged, dirty town built upon the rocks at the edge of the sea. Here we take carriages for Jerusalem, which lies up in the mountains about forty miles away. There is now a railroad from Jaffa to Jerusalem, but the carriage ride is pleasanter, for every foot of Palestine is historic ground, and its scenes are among the most interesting of all Asia.

The road is smooth and hard. Near Jaffa it is lined with orange groves, and we drive through these out upon the plains of Sharon, where the Philistines lived in the days of Goliath and David. Our road goes through flat meadows on which fat cattle are grazing. The grass is as green as that of our fields in June, and it is spotted with thousands of poppies, the flowers of which are as big as the palm of your hand, and as red as blood.

"We land at Jaffa--"

In some places the farmers are plowing. We see that the plows are made of two sticks of wood, one set into the other at almost right angles, and that the farmer holds the plow by one hand while he carries a goad in the other. Now we pass a couple of camels hitched to a plow, the proud, ungainly beasts stalking across the fields with a sullen air, as though they felt the humiliation of their labor.

On the hillsides are dark-faced shepherds watching their

flocks; and there in the field, pulling up bunches of grass for her cattle, is a girl who makes us think of Ruth gathering wheat in the harvest fields of Boaz. The plains of Sharon are the richest part of Palestine, and we do not wonder that the Philistines fought for them.

"— a couple of camels hitched to a plow

It takes us a half day to reach the hills upon which the Israelites lived. The road winds in and out among little mountains. We pass groves of olive trees, and, climbing higher and higher, we come at last to the little plateau upon which the city of Jerusalem stands.

Before we enter the city, let us take a bird's-eye view of Palestine. Its size is a surprise to us. We knew that it was small, but we did not think how very small it is. Palestine is not, on the average, more than fifty miles wide, and it is about one hundred and fifty miles long. Were there a railroad across it, a fast express train could go from one side to the other in an hour, and if the road ran lengthwise we might start at the north at eight o'clock in the morning, and by noon reach the other end of the country.

Just opposite Jerusalem, not a mile from the walls, is the Mount of Olives, which is twenty-seven hundred feet high. We can stand on this mountain, and on a bright day can behold the Mediterranean on the right hand, and on the left the Dead Sea and the river Jordan. It is not so far from Dan to Beersheba as from New York to Washington, and the Jordan is so narrow that almost any boy could throw a stone across most parts of it. The country is rocky and at present mostly barren and uncultivated.

Ancient Palestine.

Jerusalem is surrounded by hills covered with limestone. The walls of the city are of yellow limestone, beautifully cut, and of the height of a four-story house. They run around the town, skirting the edges of a little plateau. From three sides of this plateau the ground slopes down into valleys at an angle so steep that it is almost impossible to climb up without getting down on your hands and knees. The fourth side of the city faces a plain.

The space inside the walls is covered with a mass of boxlike limestone houses, built one on top of the other and crowded along narrow streets in all sorts of shapes. Above them here and there rises the spire of a church, and at one corner of the city there is a space of thirty-five

The River Jordan, Palestine.

acres, in which stands an immense round building with a dome of bronze. This is the Mosque of Omar, which is built on the site of Solomon's Temple, and under which scientists suppose the ruins of the temple to be.

In the center of the city, rising out from among the stone boxes, may be seen another great dome. This crowns the Church of the Holy Sepulcher, and is supposed to cover the spot on which Christ was crucified. In it is kept the marble tomb in which the Oriental Christians think the body of Jesus was laid.

The remainder of Jerusalem is made up of the narrowest streets walled with houses more closely packed together than those of any other city of the world. There are more than forty thousand inhabitants, and the area of the city is less than a square mile. There are families of Jews, Greeks, and Armenians, each living in one small room — so small, indeed, that it would be thought hardly large enough for a bedroom in America.

Many of the houses have no windows, the rooms being vaulted caves, floored, walled, and ceiled with stone, and lighted only from the front. Such houses often stand one on top of the other. We visit parts of Jerusalem in which a half dozen families are packed into a like number of rooms about a little court upon which the rooms open. They are so small that their owners cannot cook in them, and the cooking is generally done in the court.

The roofs of the Jerusalem houses are flat, and not a few of them are covered with grass. They form the evening loafing places of many families, and in warm weather the people often sleep upon them. There are no chimneys, the fuel used being charcoal, which does not make much smoke.

The streets of Jerusalem are as queer as the houses.

They are narrow and winding. In some places the houses are built over the streets, and often in our walk through the city we seem to be going through long lines of vaulted caves. We find in some streets that each of the caves is a shop. The shops open right out upon

— houses are built over the streets

the street. They are not large enough for the customers to enter, and hardly big enough for the shopkeeper to turn around in them.

The workshops are of the same cavelike character, and all Jerusalem looks as though it had been made by a people who had been brought up in caves and had modeled their houses after the homes of their fathers. This is so with the villages of Palestine.

Many of them are built against the sides of the hills, the hills forming the back walls of the houses.

What a wonderful variety of faces we see on the streets! There are men from all parts of the Turkish Empire, and from nearly every country of Christendom. There are pilgrims by the thousand, and the streets are filled with curious characters and costumes.

Let us take a seat on the top of one of the houses and look down on the crowd which passes below us. That dark-faced man in a long brown and white gown with red leather shoes and a yellow kerchief covering his head is a Bedouin. His face is brown and his features are kindly. Around his headdress are two thick strands of black rope which are tied about it like a crown, and he reminds us of the Arabians we saw at Aden. Next him stands a shepherd from Bethlehem in a coat of sheepskin, with a gown underneath which falls to his feet. He has a Bethlehem girl with him, and we see that her face is as fair and her features as regular as our own. Her dress is of red and green silk, and the front of her head is ornamented with rows of gold coin strung upon strings and so tied that they form a cap above her white forehead.

Shepherds from Bethlehem.

Then there are pilgrims from Russia in long coats and trousers like ours, which are worn inside of high boots. There are Arabs on donkeys, and men from the desert on camels. It is hard for us to tell which are the Mohammedans and which are the Christians, for the dress here gives us little idea of a person's religion.

There is one class of people, however, whom we cannot mistake. They are the Jews of Jerusalem. They have olive-brown faces, curved noses, and long curls of hair hanging down in front of their ears. They wear long gowns and caps bound with fur which rest flat on their heads. The fur stands out from the cap, forming a ring round it like the quills of a mad porcupine. With these men are Jewish women, who wear bright-colored dresses and cover their shoulders with flowered shawls.

And then there are Greek men with many skirts reaching from their waists to their knees. Their heads are covered with skull caps of red felt, known as fez caps, and they wear embroidered white jackets. There are men from Ethiopia with faces like jet, and men from the north whose complexions are as fair as our own. The scene is one of the strangest on the face of the earth, and in no other city can you find so many different types, representing so many different races, countries, and creeds.

XXXV. TRAVELS AMONG THE TURKS.

WE travel on horses from Jerusalem through the Holy Land northward to Damascus, one of the oldest cities of the world, and then move in caravans from one place to another, visiting the chief towns of Turkey in Asia. We meet everywhere the officers of the sultan. They demand our passports and must know just where we are going. The sultan is the despotic ruler of the Turkish Empire, which embraces Turkey in Europe, Turkey in Asia, and the Turkish provinces of Africa. The capital of the empire is Constantinople. It is situated in Europe, but the majority of the sultan's subjects live in his Asiatic territories, which are almost as large as our Southern States.

Turkey in Asia has more than sixteen million inhabitants. We think of it as the land of the Mohammedans, but it contains also many Jews and Christians. The Turks are everywhere the rulers. They came originally from central Asia, and gradually conquered the different provinces which now make up Asiatic Turkey. They adopted the religion of the Mohammedans, and for centuries they have been the leading people of this faith.

The Governor of Jerusalem is a Turk. On the plains of Sharon, over which we passed in the last chapter, there are high stone towers in which Turkish soldiers stand to watch the fields, when the crops are ripe, to see that no one gathers the grain or fruit without giving the sultan his share. The rule is that one tenth of every crop must go to the government, and that this tenth must be collected at harvest time.

The farmers of the Turkish provinces live in villages. Outside of each town there is a threshing floor to which the wheat, barley, and like grains are brought as soon as they are cut, and trodden out by oxen or donkeys.

"— there are high stone towers —"

The farmer dares not take his grain away from the threshing floor until the taxgatherer has come and taken out the sultan's tenth.

Most Turkish cities are surrounded by walls, and at the gates are stationed officials to tax everything that comes into the city for sale. During my visit to Jerusalem there were two soldiers at each gate, who collected money upon everything, even to a single chicken or a head of lettuce. At one of the gates I saw a farmer come in, bringing a load of wood on the back of a little donkey. The wood was olive roots, and there was not, all told, more than enough to fill a two-bushel basket. My guide told me that the man expected to get twenty-five cents for the load. I saw the soldiers stop him, and after a moment he handed them coins worth about three cents as a tax on the wood, after which he was allowed to pass in.

Turkish villages are little more than collections of mud huts. We shall be surprised at the poverty of the people as we pass through the country, for Turkey contains some of the richest soil of the world. The peninsula of Asia Minor is made up of high plateaus covered with fine pastures of rich grass. The sheep and goats there produce some of the finest wool in the world, and the soil is excellent for farming.

Turkish Soldiers.

East of Syria is Mesopotamia, which was the seat of some of the richest empires of the past, and in which was the great city of Babylon, where Nebuchadnezzar ruled. This country is an almost unbroken plain, well watered and very rich.

The provinces of Armenia and Kurdistan are composed of highlands, some of the plains there being more than a mile above the sea. In Armenia we find Mt. Ararat, upon which Noah's ark is said to have landed, and the Armenians have a tradition that the Garden of Eden was located in their country.

Throughout all these countries the people live in villages. The small towns of Asia Minor are made of houses of sun-dried brick. They have flat roofs, and their windows are usually only holes through the wall.

The Armenian villagers live very simply. They have little furniture, the possessions of many a family consisting of only the straw mat which covers the floor, a rude chest which contains their clothes, a few copper vessels, and some stone water jars. The cooking is done upon open fires, or in ovens of clay or stone. The floor is used for serving the meals, and the fingers of the people take the place of knives and forks.

The houses of many of the Armenian villages are built either wholly or partly under the ground. An excavation is made in the side of a hill, and the houses are built within it, so that we can hardly tell where they are unless we come to them from the front. They are of one story, and their flat roofs are covered with two or three feet of earth, on which the grass grows. There are no fences about the roofs, and we often see cattle and sheep eating grass on the tops of the houses.

The floors are usually sunk below the level of the ground, and we have to step down to go in. Upon entering we find a cow stable on one side, and on the other side the room which often forms the kitchen, parlor, and bedroom of the family. It is very cold in Armenia during the greater part of the winter, and this is why the houses are built in a cavelike manner.

We find the Turks very hospitable. At each village the ruler asks us to take dinner with him, and he is expected to offer strangers a place to stay for at least one night. If we should offer to pay for our entertainment, the Turk would be insulted.

You see few beggars in Turkey, but the poor man without a dinner often goes at mealtimes to call upon his more wealthy neighbor, and is seldom turned away. The food of the people consists of rice, millet, wheat, and different kinds of meat. They are fond of sweets, and they make delicious candies, sirups, and preserves.

Turkey has a number of large cities. Smyrna, on the Mediterranean Sea, contains about two hundred thousand people. Damascus is quite as large. Bagdad has one hundred and eighty thousand, and Aleppo has more than one hundred thousand inhabitants. In these cities live many rich merchants, who have comfortable homes. The houses of the well-to-do Turks have special quarters for the women, guests of the other sex being received in the outer apartments.

The women of Turkey are shut off by themselves, and the women's quarters of a rich Turk's house are often guarded by slaves. A Turkish woman never goes out upon the street without covering her whole form in a blue or black gown, which makes her look as though she were walking about in a balloon. In addition to this garment she has a veil over her face. On the street it is impossible to tell one woman from another, the veils being so thick that you cannot distinguish the features, nor see whether the faces are beautiful or not. The house dress consists of a pair of very full trousers and a jacket.

Turkish Woman.

Many of the Turkish men wear gowns which reach to their feet, and under these very full pantaloons. Some wear pantaloons of cloth, and short jackets much like a roundabout. The pantaloons are tied at the ankles, and the shoes below are usually turned up at the toes and are often made without heels. Many of the men's jackets are embroidered with silver and gold, and the men are, as a rule, fond of fine clothes. They have their heads shaved, with the exception of a lock on the crown, and they wear skull caps or turbans, keeping them on while in the house.

A Barber.

In Turkey husbands and wives do not eat together. They do not mix together at parties. Children are promised in marriage in infancy, and boys are encouraged to get married while they are still in their teens. There is no courting done. All marriage arrangements are made by the parents of the bride and groom. At the time of the betrothal the mother of the groom takes a present of candy to the bride. The bride bites one of the choicest bits in two, eats half of it, and sends the other half back to the young man. It is said that he usually receives it with joy as a love offering, and eats it. Weddings usually take place in the afternoon, when the bridegroom says a prayer in the presence of the bride, kneeling on her bridal veil as he does so.

The Turks are not as a rule well educated. The Mohammedan priests act as the teachers, and the mosques or

Turkish Men and Boys.

temples are often used for schoolhouses. Turkish boys sit crosslegged on wide lounges or divans, or on the floor, as they study. They hold their books on their knees and study out loud. They have no school desks, and they hold their copy books in their hands while they write. The Koran, the Mohammedan bible, forms a large part of their studies. Most of the people, it is said, learn to read and write, and every boy commits to memory the different prayers required in his religion.

The chief products of Turkey are wheat, cotton, and opium. Quite large amounts of raw silk and wool are exported. The people weave fine silks and beautiful cloths of silver and gold; and some of the most costly rugs of the world are made in Turkey. They are woven by women and girls in their homes, upon the rudest of looms. The weavers kneel or sit crosslegged at their work, several girls often working at the same rug, each taking a section of about two feet to weave.

The work is done entirely by hand, the tufts of wool being tied together and fastened into the threads without the aid of a shuttle. The rugs are finally clipped smooth with scissors. They are so woven that they are as soft as the finest of machine-made carpets, and they last very much longer. Such work is very slow. A good weaver cannot make more than three or four inches of carpet a day, and a hearth rug of the best quality, seven feet long by four feet wide, requires six months' steady work.

XXXVI. RUSSIA IN WEST ASIA.

WE take our last view of Asia in traveling through the Russian possessions on the western side of it. We recall our visit to eastern Siberia, on the northern Pacific Ocean, and here, after thousands of miles of travel in strange countries, moving through all kinds of climates and all varieties of scenery, we find ourselves again on Russian soil.

We stand amazed when we think of the possessions of Russia in Asia. They consist of the province of Trans-Caucasia (map on p. 265), the vast territories east of the Caspian Sea known as Russian Turkestan, the Kirghiz Steppes, and Siberia — embracing an area, all told, which is about twice the size of the United States.

In Trans-Caucasia we visit the city of Tiflis. It has a population of more than one hundred thousand Georgians, Armenians, and Russians. The Georgian men wear long robes gathered in by a belt at the waist, pantaloons, high boots, and cone-shaped caps of black wool or astrakhan. They have rows of cartridges upon their breasts, and carry pistols in their belts. Many of them wear swords, and they impress us by their fierce looks.

The Georgian women are very pretty and are much desired by the Turks as wives. In the past, Turkish slave traders carried on a regular business in buying these girls and shipping them to Constantinople. This is now contrary to law, but it is said that beautiful Georgian girls are still often sold by their parents to the slave traders, and are sometimes stolen and smuggled out of the country. Georgian women have fair, rosy complexions, black hair, large eyes, and white teeth. They have slender forms, with small hands and feet. They are fine dancers and are fond of music, many of them playing upon tambourines and a kind of a guitar. They wear gowns much like those of the women of Europe, and their headdress consists of a small round cap, over which is thrown a white silk or lace handkerchief tied under the chin.

We visit the Russian oil regions about the Caspian Sea. The city of Baku, on its western shore, is the great oil center. The territory about it is spotted with derricks or high frameworks for the pumping of petroleum, and it reminds us of the scenes in the oil regions of Pennsylvania.

At Baku we get a steamer which takes us across the Caspian Sea and lands us on the opposite shore, and thence by a land journey we come to the great Trans-Caspian railroad, which carries us nearly a thousand miles into the heart of central Asia. Both the engines of the steamer and those which pull our cars use petroleum as fuel.

We travel for miles through deserts, visiting now and then an oasis, or fertile spot, where the land is cut up by irrigating canals and every drop of water is saved to feed the thirsty soil.

We pass through the little countries of Khiva and Bokhara, peopled by Tartars who raise wheat, rice, barley, cotton, tobacco, and silk. We find delicious peaches, melons, and grapes. The railroad takes us through vast fields of cotton, the seed of which was brought from America, and the product of which is now competing with our cotton in the markets of Russia. We see tribes of wandering Tartars, who live in tents and look not unlike the Turks we saw in Turkey. This region was the original home of the Turks, and from here they moved westward to the countries along the Mediterranean Sea.

Siberian Farmers.

The land rises as we go to the east. We reach the Pamir (pameer'), which is one of the highest countries of the world, and then move northward on a high plateau through Russian Turkestan on our way to Siberia. Passing between the great bodies of salt water known as the Aral Sea and Lake Balkash, we travel over the Kirghiz Steppes and meet the Tartar herders and shepherds who form its inhabitants. They are known as Kirghiz, and they are one of the most numerous of the nomad races of Asia. There are more than three millions of them, and their country is more than a third as large as Russia in Europe.

The Kirghiz have vast numbers of camels, sheep, horses, and cows. They think it is more respectable to live in tents and to move about from one pasture field to another, than to live in towns, and they are proud of being stock breeders rather than farmers.

They remind us much of our American Indians, and we find them not unlike the Tartars whom we saw north of the Great Wall of China. They have high cheek bones, small, oblique eyes, and complexions which are almost the color of copper. Both men and women wear yellow or red leather trousers fastened at the waist with a girdle. Over these they have long robes much like dressing gowns tied in by a belt at the waist. The women wear a close-fitting shirt in addition to their trousers and robe.

The Kirghiz are Mohammedans, but the women do not cover their faces so carefully as in other Mohammedan countries. They are fond of jewelry. They paint and powder their faces, and braid ribbon and horsehair into their locks in order to make their hair appear longer.

The Kirghiz have some curious marriage customs. Girls are married at the age of fifteen, and at twenty-three an unmarried girl is looked upon as an old maid. The groom has to pay a certain amount to the parents of the bride before the marriage can take place. This payment is generally in the form of sheep, horses, or camels. A poor and rather homely girl is often sold for one or two camels, but the beautiful daughter of a rich man may bring as much as one hundred sheep or fifty camels.

The Kirghiz men allow their wives to do the most of the work. The women put up and take down the tents and load them upon the camels when the family moves from one place to another. They aid in watching the stock, and they are expected to do all the milking. This, among the Kirghiz, is a great task, for not only the cows, but also sheep, goats, and mares are milked.

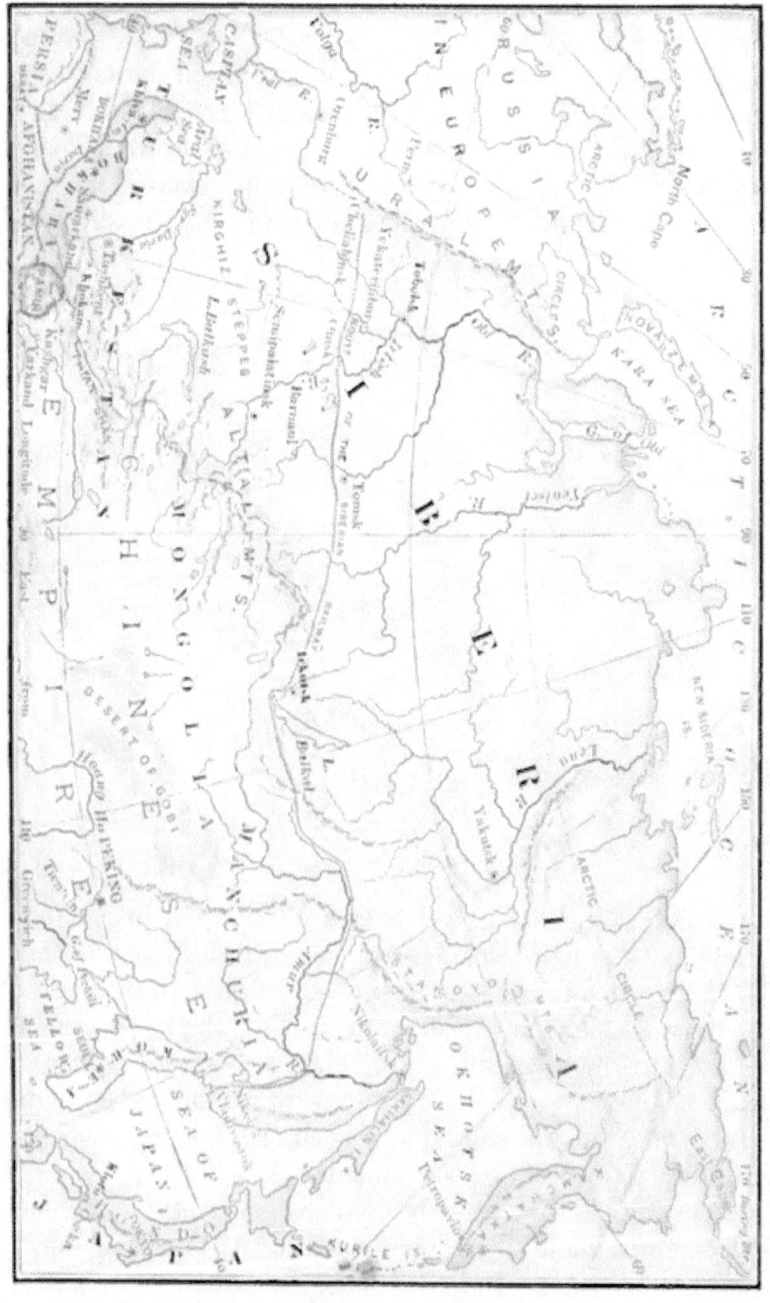

Cows, sheep, and goats are milked only in the morning and evening, but the mares are milked three times a day. One of the greatest dainties among the Kirghiz is made from mare's milk. It is a kind of liquor known as koumiss, which is made by putting the milk into a leather bag and keeping it there for about two weeks, during which time it is now and then stirred and shaken. It soon ferments

mares are milked.

and produces a liquor which tastes somewhat like buttermilk, but which, if too much is taken, will make one drunk.

Just north of the Kirghiz Steppes lies western Siberia. It consists, to a large extent, of an unbroken plain, some of which is made up of bog and swamp, but a great part of which is fertile soil. It is watered by the great rivers Obi and Irtish, and its southern portion will at some time in the future support a vast population.

Western Siberia already contains about three million inhabitants, more than ninety per cent. of whom have come from Russia and are engaged in farming, stock raising, and mining. The remainder are native Siberians who are hunters and laborers.

We find but few towns, and no very large cities in Siberia. The capital is Irkutsk, which contains about forty thousand people, and which, though so far away from Europe, has excellent schools, a museum, a theater, a library, and a good hotel.

Irkutsk reminds us of home. Its outskirts have log houses like those of our pioneer towns, but the buildings on the main streets are of brick and stone. Were it not

Plowing in Siberia.

for the Russian characters on the signboards, some of the stores would not seem out of place in America. Many of them have plate-glass windows, and upon entering we find all sorts of goods which have been imported from Europe. We meet women on the streets whose dresses are not unlike those of our mothers at home, and it seems good to find again men wearing hats, coats, shirts, and pantaloons, instead of turbans and gowns.

Irkutsk is on the line of the Trans-Siberian railroad,

far in the interior of southern Siberia. We move along the line surveyed for the road to the westward, finding the Russians at work in many places, until we at last reach the western section of the railroad, which goes from Omsk to the town of Cheliabinsk in the Ural Mountains.

A large part of the western section has been completed, and we soon come to the cars and finish our tour of Asia by steaming into Cheliabinsk. We are now at the western end of the great Trans-Siberian railroad, and as we stand in the Ural Mountains we can in our minds look back across Siberia along this trunk line and see the point at which we first visited it, at Vladivostok on the Pacific. We learn that the main line of the road, 4696 miles long, will cost the enormous sum of one hundred and seventy-five million dollars, and that it will be completed in the year 1905. We see that through it southern Siberia will sometime become one of the richest and most populous countries of the world, and we are more and more struck with the vast area and riches of the country.

We see more of the Russians as we take a rapid flight by rail through Russia to Germany. Fast trains carry us to Moscow and St. Petersburg. After a short stay at the capital of the czar, we go by rail to Berlin, and thence to Hamburg, where we get a steamer for the United States. The passage across the Atlantic requires only seven days, and within a week after sailing we find ourselves again on American soil in the city of New York.

www.ingramcontent.com/pod-product-compliance
Lightning Source LLC
Chambersburg PA
CBHW021159230426
43667CB00006B/472